THE WILD GOD OF THE WORLD

The Wild God of the World

AN ANTHOLOGY OF

Robinson Jeffers

Selected, with an Introduction, by

ALBERT GELPI

Stanford University Press

STANFORD, CALIFORNIA 2003

STANFORD UNIVERSITY PRESS   Stanford, California

Printed in the United States of America on acid-free, archival-quality paper

Library of Congress Cataloging-in-Publication Data
Jeffers, Robinson, 1887–1962.
  The wild god of the world : an anthology of Robinson Jeffers /
  selected, with an introduction, by Albert Gelpi.
     p.   cm.
  Includes index.
  ISBN 0-8047-4591-9 (alk. paper) — ISBN 0-8047-4592-7 (pbk. : alk. paper)
     I. Gelpi, Albert.   II. Title.
  PS3519.E27   A6   2003
  811'.52—dc21
  2002153166

Designed and typeset by Jeff Clark at Wilsted & Taylor Publishing Services in 11.5/13 Centaur, following Adrian Wilson's original design for *The Collected Poetry of Robinson Jeffers*

Original Printing 2003

Last figure below indicates year of this printing:
11   10   09   08   07   06   05   04   03

CONTENTS

PROSE

PREFACE

The five-volume *Collected Poetry* from the Stanford University Press, edited by Tim Hunt, is the lasting monument to Robinson Jeffers' poetic achievement. This anthology, drawn from that master text, has a different but complementary purpose; it serves as an introduction to Jeffers' work for the general reader and for students in courses on American poetry. It was Jeffers' custom to compose each volume of verse with one or two long narrative or dramatic poems as its center and a constellation of shorter lyric or meditative poems as emotional and philosophical context. In structuring *The Wild God of the World*, I have followed this practice of Jeffers.

Cawdor, one of Jeffers' most powerful narratives, really a novelette in verse, first published in the 1928 volume of that title, is at the center of the volume and is surrounded by a representative selection of shorter poems from a career of more than four decades. I took as my title a phrase that sums up the pantheism underlying all Jeffers' work; it comes from "Hurt Hawks," a personal lyric included in this collection and thematically linked to *Cawdor*. In addition, I have provided at the end Jeffers' revealing statements about his poetry and poetics and about the philosophy of nature and human nature that informs his life's work. My aim has been to put into readers' hands, in a single, compact but wide-ranging volume, all they need for engaging Jeffers' poetic world, at once epic and tragic, prophetic and sublime, intimate and apocalyptic.

I am acutely and gratefully aware of the many scholars and critics whose work has made this volume possible. I especially want to mention Tim Hunt's magisterial editing of the *Collected Poems*; the biographical investigations of James Karman and Lawrence Clark Powell; and the critical insights of Robert Brophy, Robert Zaller, and William Everson. Everson came to a sense of his own poetic vocation through Jeffers' verse, and although he pursued his own quite different course in life and poetry, he continued to acknowledge and acclaim the master he never met. Besides his elegy for Jeffers, "The Poet Is Dead," he wrote two pioneering critical books on the poetry, edited two books of Jeffers' early verse and a reissuing of *Cawdor* and *Medea* in a double volume, and designed and printed on his hand press a magnificent book of Jeffers' poems under the title *Granite and Cypress*. Bill Everson was also, to me, a loving and much loved friend as well as a powerful poet. I dedicate *The Wild God of the World* to his memory.

ALBERT GELPI
Stanford, California
May 27, 2002

INTRODUCTION

Robinson Jeffers and the Sublime

I

Robinson Jeffers is a major figure in that extraordinary generation of Americans who dominated poetry in the first half of the twentieth century; his compatriots included Ezra Pound, T. S. Eliot, Wallace Stevens, Marianne Moore, William Carlos Williams, and H. D. Jeffers maintained fierce guard over his independence and privacy from his fastness on the Pacific coast, but the publication of *Tamar* in 1924, followed by *Roan Stallion, Tamar and Other Poems* the next year, suddenly made him a public figure and something of a *cause célèbre* because of the violence and sexuality of those narratives. He was hailed or condemned, but in either case recognized as a new and primal force in poetry. As a result, he had larger sales and a wider audience than Pound, Eliot, or any of the others with their Modernist *avant-garde* coterie of readers. The apex of his national fame is marked by his picture on the cover of *Time* for April 4, 1932: rugged and handsome face in profile, outlined against the granite wall of his house, a cool sidewise swipe of a glance at once searching out and holding off the viewer.

In the thirties and forties, however, Jeffers seemed increasingly out of step politically and poetically. He dismissed the social realism and proletarian politics of the Depression years, and his isolationist opposition to America's entry into the Second World War put him in a very small minority during the national dedication to winning what came to be called the "good war." Moreover, as Modernism and New Critical formalism were adopted by the critical establishment and the academy, Jeffers found himself labeled an outdated and unfashionable Romantic. The decline in Jeffers' reputation was matched by the literary canonization of Eliot, Pound, Stevens, Moore, and finally Williams and H. D.; during his last years and after his death, Jeffers' isolation became its own distinction, zealously guarded and celebrated by a committed circle of defenders.

The process of reconsideration, however, has begun to move discussion beyond the crossed trajectories of Modernist and anti-Modernist to a more accurate assessment of Jeffers' place in twentieth-century poetry. He has to be understood as part of his generation, precisely in his opposition to many of its dominant tendencies; indeed, his opposition serves to clarify not only the scope and limits of his position but also the scope and limits of the Modernist position. For Jeffers, as for his fellows, the crisis facing them was finding not just a voice but even a ground for speaking in a civilization headed for catastrophe without the religious, moral, or political conviction to avert disaster, much less to envision a better world. For Jeffers — as for Eliot, Pound, Stevens, and H. D. — World War I was the defining event: the beginning of the end for which Oswald Spengler's *The Decline of the West* was but one prophetic voice. For him, as for them, the Second World War was the next fateful act in the tragedy. If Modernism was bracketed and defined by the two wars, so was Jeffers' anti-Modernism.

Jeffers began writing poetry as a boy and by his teenage years was taking himself seriously as a poet, although he would not come into his own until the years just after World War I. His first mature narrative, *Tamar*, was written in 1922, the year that saw the publication of Eliot's *The Waste Land*, the paradigmatic Modernist poem, and Joyce's *Ulysses*, the paradigmatic Modernist novel. But *Tamar* left no doubt that Jeffers was deliberately setting a course that dismissed and challenged the Modernist aesthetic. The poets whose work by his own account had saturated his sensibility were Romantic and Victorian: Shelley, Rossetti, Swinburne, Tennyson, early Yeats; among earlier poets, he singled out Milton and Marlowe. All these poets, by Modernist standards, were too rich and ripe in their emotional, rhetorical, and metaphorical excesses; for Modernists, the declension from Shelley to Rossetti to the Yeats of the Celtic Twilight traces the decadence of nineteenth-century Romanticism. But when Jeffers read Pound and Eliot, Rimbaud, and Mallarmé, he found in the Modernist experiments — the fracturing of form, the impersonal submersion or splintering of the poetic voice, the choice of abstraction and incoherence and indeterminacy — not just an elitist disregard for the reading audience but, even more alarmingly, a self-defeating capitulation to the very conditions of modernity that were the besetting problem. Jeffers' narratives and dramas, with their chronological plots and strongly delineated characters as well as the lyric "I" of his shorter poems, were deliberate aesthetic choices to counter the dominant mode. In his undeviating view, Modernism was not the solution to the disintegration of Romanticism but the manifestation and completion of that disintegration. His life-and-death response was to resist Modernism by reconstituting the Romantic sense of the divinity of nature for the twentieth century to redeem modernity from its own doomed proclivities.

Jeffers' poetry, then, arose out of a radical sense of psychological, moral, and spiritual crisis with the purpose of meeting that crisis. The subsequent sections of this introduction examine the unfolding of his poetic course biographically, thematically, and formally.

2

In his late poem "Patronymic," Jeffers looks back to a Scot or Welsh progenitor named "Godfrey," "which means the peace of God." The poem traces the genealogy from Godfrey through "Geoffrey, Jeffry's son, Jeffries" to "Jeffers in Ireland" (*Selected Poetry*, 686). By the early nineteenth century, Joseph Jeffers emigrated from County Monaghan to rural Ohio. His son, William Hamilton Jeffers, married Annie Robinson Tuttle, twenty-two years his junior, in 1885. Their first child, John Robinson Jeffers, was born in Pittsburgh, Pennsylvania, on January 10, 1887. Robin, as he was called by family and later by friends, was adored by his parents, and to the end he remained very close to both.

Jeffers' parents both had been raised in the Covenanter church, a Calvinist denomination, and they met when Rev. Dr. Jeffers was serving as temporary pastor in a Presbyterian church where Annie played the organ. One of her forebears was Jonathan Edwards, the great Calvinist theologian and Puritan divine. Dr. Jeffers had graduated from Xenia Theological Seminary and been ordained a Presbyterian minister in 1859. After service in the Civil War, he pursued an academic career in appointments to a series of seminaries in the Pittsburgh area. He became professor of Latin and Hebrew at Westminster College in 1865, professor of Greek at Wooster College in 1869, and professor of Old Testament, Biblical and Ecclesiastical History and History of Doctrine at Western Theological Seminary from 1877 to 1903.

These details about Jeffers' parents are significant because the close-knit household in which he was reared and educated shaped his mind and spirit for the rest of his life. He grew up in a family in which the Presbyterian Shorter Catechism was to be committed to heart and memory but in which religious faith and strict observance were combined with a love of languages, history, and literature. Jeffers remembered that his father's temperament and domestic rule allowed almost no contact and certainly no comradeship with other children. Even within the family, the seven years that separated him from his younger brother Hamilton left him to himself with all the time he wanted to read and write and daydream. By his teenage years, the boy was a prodigy who knew German and French as well as Hebrew, Greek, and Latin; he studied literature and history, with an emphasis on the classical and the medieval, in private schools in Pittsburgh and abroad (with his doting mother in residence nearby). He continued to pursue these passions after the family moved to Pasadena in 1902, at Occidental College (from which he graduated at age eighteen), and then at the University of Southern California.

In his elegy "To His Father," the poet acknowledges that he "followed other guides" than the Christ who had been Dr. Jeffers' "lord and captain." But the sensibility of the son was informed by his parents, especially by the austere and intellectual man who was almost fifty when he became a father and yet combined the authority of theologian and preacher with a proud and nurturing love for his son. Jeffers' narratives and dramas take as their sources the texts he first learned in his carefully nurtured education at home and in school: Greek epic and tragedy, the Hebrew Bible, and the Gospels. As a result, the tragic sense and prophetic intent of Jeffers' poetry are fired by a fierce Protestant piety and an imagination unerringly Calvinist in its sense of the Godhead as *deus absconditus*, sublimely above and beyond unredeemably self-willed, ego-driven humans.

The other person who became a determining presence in Jeffers' poetry was Una Call Kuster. She and Jeffers met and fell in love immediately in 1906 at the University of Southern California. He was doing graduate work studying oratory and languages, including Old English, and she was pursuing her love of philosophy and literature as a refuge from the country club atmosphere of her unhappy marriage to the successful Los Angeles lawyer Edward Kuster. Her master's thesis on *The Enduring Element of Mysticism in Man* indicates the spiritual and philosophical affinities that underlay their passion for each other and for poetry. The period between their meeting and their marriage seven years later was a time of testing and searching for both. Jeffers traveled to Zurich to study in the summer of 1906, immersed himself for two years in medical study at USC, and in the fall of 1910 began an academic year in the School of Forestry at the University of Washington (with his devoted parents moving up to Seattle to provide him a home). These erratic ventures were at least in part efforts to break the spell that drew him to the married Una, but his return to Los Angeles confirmed their commitment to each other, and it endured through Una's year of trial separation in Europe. Jeffers was waiting, more and more anxiously, for his personal and poetic life to find its course. *Flagon and Apples*, his first collection, was privately published in 1912; but he knew he had to move beyond those derivative and immature poems, and he sensed that that emergence would be connected with Una.

The first break came in 1913: Una's divorce from Kuster, sensationalized in the *Los Angeles Times* of March 1 under the headlines "Two Points of the Eternal Triangle." A sub-headline claimed that "Parents Wash Hands of It," but in fact Jeffers and Una married on August 2nd with his parents' blessing. Very soon, however, their life together suffered a succession of shocks. Their daughter Maeve, born on May 5, 1914, died the next day, and Dr. Jeffers was mortally stricken by a stroke in December of that year. Moreover, this personal grief was compounded by the public alarm at the outbreak of World War I, which many read, in James Karman's words, as "the end of Western civilization," of "Greco-Roman humanism and Judeo-Christian spirituality" (Karman, 41). However, that same terrible year saw an event that would determine the rest of Robin and Una's lives: between Maeve's death and the death of his father, they moved to Carmel-by-the-Sea, then a village just south of Monterey, California. As he would later acknowledge, "we had come without knowing it to our inevitable place" (Powell, 24).

Jeffers and Una began life in Carmel beneficently with the birth of twin sons, Donnan and Garth, in November 1916 and with the publication of his second collection, *Californians*, earlier in the year. But the final resolution of their domestic lives and the simultaneous emergence of Jeffers in the full command of his voice and medium came only after the Armistice. After living in town for five years, they bought a plot of land two miles south and around the bay from what was then the residential limits of Carmel. Their land faced the sky and sea about fifty yards above a small beach, where the surf broke around granite stones and boulders. Jeffers became an apprentice to a local stone mason, and together they began to build Tor House from stones from the beach. The cottage consisted of a living room (with a hearth and books, including volumes of Wordsworth, Shelley, and Byron lining the paneled walls); a small guest bedroom, where years later first Una and then Robin would meet their deaths; a kitchen; a bathroom; and sleeping quarters for all four in a loft. The house had running water, but at first it had neither electricity nor telephone. In time, Jeffers planted some two thousand trees in and around his property. In 1920, in the garden that Una was establishing around the house, Jeffers began the construction of Hawk Tower as her special place. Its four floors, with dungeon, secret staircase, and battlements, were completed by 1925. Over the years, Jeffers added rooms to Tor House with the help of Donnan and Garth, whom he had trained during their boyhood to work with stones. The family, as close-knit as Jeffers' own family had been, had found their rooted place and made it theirs.

The number of poems about the house and its construction, many of them included in this selection, attests to the correlation between house building and poem making. The famous poem "To the Stone-Cutters" depicts the poet as stonecutter, and raising the house made manifest the impulse for working with words. Bollingen was the stone house that the psychologist Carl Jung had built in Zurich on Lake Geneva as the symbol of his life and work, and a stone carved with a motto stood in its courtyard as the omphalos. For Jung, elemental stone, incised with the words of individual experience, symbolized the realized self. Yeats, the living master with whom Jeffers felt closest affinity, had acquired the stone tower of Thoor Ballyllee as his totemic home and wrote of it again and again; the Jefferses would visit it on one of their trips to Ireland. But Jeffers' own engagement with the granite rocks and boulders was hands-on, as he himself grappled, lifted, and fitted them into form in a labor that extended over many years. So it is not surprising that he was transformed by what he calls, in "Rock and Hawk," "the massive // Mysticism of stone." Una would describe the transformation as a conversion experience: "some kinship" with the place and with the granite he handled revealed "strengths in himself unknown before" in an "awakening such as adolescents and religious converts are said to experience" (*Selected Letters*, 213). To be specific, the gestalt of stone gave him the voice and words, the form and images to explore his pantheistic view of nature and his inhumanist view of human nature in an explosive outburst of narratives and lyrics. *Tamar and Other Poems* (1924) was its first issue; it caused a sensation and was followed by nine other volumes in the next dozen years.

Through it all, Una was herself the ground and air, the matrix and inspiration of Jeffers' creations in stone and words: wife, mother, muse, anima. This marriage of two strong, passionate people — he reserved and phlegmatic, she volatile and emotive — had periods of stress and distress. There were short-lived infidelities and jealousies, and the nadir came in 1938 during the last of their several sojourns at Mabel Dodge Luhan's ranch in Taos, New Mexico. Una discovered that her hostess was scheming to arrange an affair between Robin and another guest, and although it is unclear how serious the dalliance was, Una, angry and hurt, attempted suicide with his revolver. But she survived, and the marriage survived. They returned to Tor House to resume their lives together; the abiding bond between them absorbed even this shock and, if anything, deepened in the years left to them.

Jeffers' *Selected Poetry* appeared at the end of that same year. In his dedication and in the foreword (included in this volume), he chose to affirm publicly his allegiance to and symbiotic dependence on Una:

> My nature is cold and undiscriminating; she focussed and excited it, gave it eyes and nerves and sympathies. She never saw any of my poems until it was finished and typed, yet by her presence and conversation she has co-authored every one of them. Sometimes I think there must be some value in them, if only for that reason. She is more like a woman in a Scotch ballad, passionate, untamed, and rather heroic — or like a falcon — than like an ordinary person.

William Carlos Williams said the poet was the woman in him, and many male poets have come to identify their creativity with their feminine aspect, what Jung called the *anima*. In Jeffers' imagination, Una, whose very name suggested some single and all-embracing force, was his living and sustaining link with nature. She functioned as the objective correlative of the capabilities "unknown before" his early twenties, and his union with her mediated between his consciousness and the preconscious and superconscious energies animate in the universe. As testament to her empowerment, he had built her tower in stone so that from its foundations in earth it rose up to the sky like the hawk or falcon that was her totem in nature. His recentering on Una after the terrible episode in Taos found further expression in the sequence "For Una" in his next volume, *Be Angry at the Sun* (1941).

In September 1939, the war that had been gathering momentum since the botched armistice of 1918 broke over the world like Armageddon. For Jeffers, violence was the human condition, the inevitable consequence of the aggressive ego aggrandized into national ego. "Shine, Perishing Republic" had issued a prophetic warning in the *Tamar* volume of 1924, and in the *Solstice* volume of 1935, "Shine Republic" redacted the warning in the hope of staving off another disaster. Like Pound, expatriate in Italy, Jeffers saw World War II as the clash between vast and contending blocks of political and economic power and so opposed U. S. participation in the war. Jeffers' stance met with angry disfavor, but, for several reasons, Jeffers did not share Pound's fate of being charged with treason. He was speaking from home territory rather than from an enemy country, and although he attacked beloved leaders like

Roosevelt and Churchill, he did not link his opposition to fascist or anti-Semitic sympathies as Pound did. Moreover, the virulence of his views became fully clear only with the publication of *The Double Axe* in 1948. Random House issued that volume only with certain poems censored and excised and with a notice at the front disassociating the publisher from the political views contained therein. (Tim Hunt reviews the vexed question of the text of and omissions from the 1948 *Double Axe* in volume III of the *Collected Poems*.)

Before the storm over *The Double Axe*, however, Jeffers had scored a great popular success with his rendition of Euripides' *Medea*, written for his friend, actress Judith Anderson. The text was published in 1946, and the Broadway production with Anderson in the lead played with great acclaim to enthusiastic audiences in a run that extended from October 1947 to May 1948. In the flush of this acclamation, *The New York Times* invited a statement from him, and he took the occasion to sum up his poetics in the essay "Poetry, Gongorism, and a Thousand Years," appearing in *The New York Times Magazine* for January 18, 1948, and included in this volume.

Suddenly mortality began to close in on Jeffers, however. During the summer of 1948, he almost died in Ireland of a strep infection that had heart complications, and recovery was slow through a long convalescence. Then early the next year, Una was diagnosed with a recurrence of the cancer for which she had been treated five years before. She carried on bravely, with him in attendance, until her death in his arms at Tor House on September 1, 1950. He was devastated by the loss but persisted for another dozen years, living in the now much enlarged house with Donnan and his wife Lee and their children. He was able to put together the volume *Hungerfield* (1954) with the beautiful elegy "The Deer Lay Down Their Bones" and with an invocation to Una opening the long title narrative. In the late twenties, "The Bed by the Window" had anticipated his death, and he met it there on January 20, 1962. The following year, a posthumous volume, *The Beginning and the End*, gathered the last poems: no long narrative but a number of extraordinary lyrics in which he faces death with serene equanimity and stoic acquiescence.

3

The religious and philosophical convictions that drive Jeffers' poetry from *Tamar* to the end can be summed up under twin headings: pantheism and inhumanism. The interaction and tension between these positions provide the ongoing drama of all his work. In Jeffers, as William Everson put it, "the latent American pantheistic seed," which had its first poetic flowering with Emerson and Whitman in the mid-nineteenth century, "had found its Californian fertility, and a new breed was born" (Everson, viii). A new Californian strain of American pantheism: and what made the difference between Jeffers and Emerson or Whitman — both enthusiastic humanists — was the philosophical stance that by the forties Jeffers was explicitly calling inhumanism.

Jeffers' utter disillusionment with human nature was rooted in his Calvinist agnosticism: Calvinism without Christ, without God's redemptive incarnation in the human condition. In Christian theology, original sin symbolizes the breach opened and perpetuated between creation and the Creator by the rebelliousness of the human ego and will. God's assumption of the human condition in the person of Jesus to redeem His sinful creatures makes the Incarnation the central Christian tenet and mystery. But Calvinist theology represents historically the extreme of the Protestant Reformation of Catholic belief and practice. It posits a schism between the human and divine so radical as to be almost absolute. On the one side, the innate depravity of humans makes them unworthy of salvation and incapable of doing anything to merit it, and on the other side the Creator is the *deus absconditus*, the hidden God, withdrawn from human apprehension and from human concerns and conflicts. For Calvinists, God can and does elect to save certain of His self-damned creatures through the agency of Jesus, but the doctrine of divine election so narrows and constricts the operancy of the Incarnation as to focus the Calvinist consciousness on sin rather than grace, on damnation rather than on salvation.

"I know that He exists / Somewhere in silence," Emily Dickinson begins one of her poems. In all the obvious ways, Dickinson is as far removed from Jeffers as her Amherst is removed, in time and culture and a continent's space, from Jeffers' Carmel coast. Neither is a Calvinist in intellectual adherence. But what she shared with Jeffers, and what they both did not share with Emerson and Whitman, is the persistence of engrained and unquestioned assumptions and responses that constitute the Calvinist imagination beyond adherence to its tenets as a creed. In his play *Dear Judas* (1929), Jeffers portrays Jesus as a high-minded and well-meaning teacher whose doomed mission to save humankind through a gospel of love is based on his deluded sense that he is the Son of God. After Jeffers lost faith in his father's God, he understood Euripides' tragedies but not Dante's divine comedy. His unassuageable conviction of undeniable and deserved doom found confirmation in his readings in the materialist cosmology of the Roman poet Lucretius, the biology of Darwin, the pessimistic philosophy of Nietzsche, and the apocalyptic history of Spengler.

Emerson was not a Christian, but his optimistic and transcendental reading of evolution, derived from Laplanck, posited a spiritual agency governing the progressive spiral of material existence up and back to its Creator. Emerson was in fact a transcendentalist, not a pantheist, precisely because for him, as he says in his manifesto *Nature* (1836), "Nature is symbol of spirit," and so physical / biological laws function as the visible manifestation of metaphysical laws. Jeffers' materialist sense of evolution posited only the chance mutations of biological adaptation and saw the development of the human species as an evolutionary mischance in which ego consciousness, its distinctive trait, pits human beings against the harmonious integrity of natural process. Emerson's intuition of the primacy of Spirit could sometimes make him experience material existence as merely, in the Hindu word, *maya*, illusion. But Jeffers' poem "Credo" scoffs at such mind-centered idealism: "The beauty of things was born before eyes and sufficient to itself; the heart-breaking beauty / Will remain when there is no heart to break for it." Jeffers was a true pantheist because his God was the life and law, the integrity and harmony of biological and material existence: in the words from "Hurt Hawks," "the wild God of the world."

The focus of Calvinism was, as we have seen, not on the Incarnate Christ but on the Father as *deus absconditus*, the sublime Other *beyond* nature and human nature. Christ was "the narrow gate" through which the predestined elect were delivered from nature and history. The great Protestant theologian Karl Barth, in redacting Calvinism for the twentieth century, observed that Christ's "greatest achievement is a negative achievement" in that it sacrifices material human existence "to the incomparably Greater and the invisibly Other" (Lynch, 31; Barth, 97). However, Jeffers' pantheism shifted the terms of the Calvinist declension further. By denying the Incarnation, Jeffers closed the narrow gate and put God utterly outside human history. Then, by identifying transcendent divinity with natural process, he confirmed an absolute breach between nature and humanity and excluded humans from any communion with "the wild God of the world" in its dynamic wholeness and perfection.

Jeffers' reading in science and psychology confirmed his conviction that consciousness, which Christians like Dante and humanists like Emerson took to be the distinguishing and crowning glory of humans, was in fact the original sin that separated us from the divine processes of nature. The Dickinson poem that begins "A loss of something ever felt I" posits the first moment of consciousness as the moment of bereavement. The awareness of self involves a distinction *from* others, splitting the Me from the Not-Me: from other men and women, from nature, from God, in Jeffers' terms, from nature as God. Consciousness, by coming into itself, falls instantly and inescapably into self-consciousness, navelled on a fragile, vulnerable ego driven to self-protection and self-assertion by its own insatiable anxieties and inexhaustible needs.

In Jeffers' own words from the original "Preface" to *The Double Axe*, the "mental processes" of the alienated and self-alienated individual "continually distort and prevent each other, so that his energy is devoted to introversion and the civil wars of the mind." Consequently, contact with the world outside can only mean conflict. Instead of engagement with and participation in the natural world, the egoist expends himself in "self-interference, self-frustration, self-incitement, self-tickling, self-worship" (*Selected Poetry*, 719–20). As a further consequence, his selfish contact with other equally alienated men and women ends in violence and violation: physical, sexual, moral, spiritual. No wonder the plots of the narratives and dramas tangle and snarl the characters into destruction and self-destruction, and no wonder narcissism and incest are often the twinned sins.

The source of *Cawdor*, the title poem of Jeffers' 1928 volume and the narrative at the heart of this anthology, is not biblical but classical: the story, told by Euripides and others, of Phaedra's hopeless and unrequited passion for Hippolytus, the innocent and youthful hunter—son (by a previous marriage) of her older husband, King Theseus. In his "Foreword" to the 1938 *Selected Poetry*, Jeffers said that the California coast from Carmel down to Big Sur was a location comparable to "Homer's Ithaca" and so comparable in its heroic and tragic possibilities: "Here was life purged of its ephemeral accretions. Men were riding after cattle, or plowing the headland, hovered by white sea- gulls, as they have done for thousands of years, and will for thousands of years to come." But this was no Wordsworthian pastoral. Although on the Carmel coast contemporary life transpires close to the "permanent life" of rock and sea and hawk, it is still "not shut from the modern world"; the advantage is rather that it expresses the modern dilemma "unencumbered by the mass of poetically irrelevant details and complexities" that plague urban civilization. Thus, when the characters in his narrative and dramatic poems tower in their elemental directness and even crudity above the characters in realist fiction and drama, they express the human condition in terms as large and harsh and extreme as that condition warrants. And under the violent stress, epic breaks into tragedy, for although Jeffers admitted to reading Freud and Jung in the twenties, the passions of his characters rage with an unchecked and single-minded ferocity that owes more to Aeschylus and Euripides than to Freud.

Jeffers' Phedra is Fera, married out of economic need to the aging and widowed patriarch–rancher Cawdor but consumed with lust for his chaste hunter–son Hood. And Fera is one of many passionate and strong-willed women characters behind whom the image of Una stands. The plot turns on the violent, often bloody altercations between Fera and Hood, but the narrative is named after Cawdor and ends with his Oedipus-like act of self-blinding to stress that his willful forcing of marriage on Fera was the first aggressive act that precipitated the macabre events that would bring them all down. As in all Jeffers' narratives, the human events take their terrible course against an awesome landscape of vast scale and rugged splendor. Against, in two senses: the landscape contrasts with the violence of the action, and the action desecrates the sublimity of the landscape.

Many readers of Jeffers' "sombre and God-tormented poems" (Everson, vii) find them disturbing and offensive. Understandably and rightly so: they are meant to be so jolting that they will, in the words of "Carmel Point," "uncenter our minds from ourselves, ... unhumanize our views a little" — and thus change the way we think and live. Jeffers is a prophet, and prophecy is meant to be a performative act. His words translate into human terms the reality of the transcendent power — often in challenging but intentionally transformative denunciation of the values and conduct of the prophet's hearers and readers. The prophet's message demands a conversion.

Yet how does Jeffers conceive that conversion? Prophet though he was and for that very reason, he knew more acutely than his audience the dilemma of the converted consciousness cognizant of "the wild God of the world." For how can consciousness, which separates us *from* nature and God, become consciousness *of* nature as God? The first intimation of "the wild God of the world" seems to exact the sacrifice of consciousness. And indeed Jeffers at times calls for and anticipates the extinction of the self-destructive human species as the only and necessary way to restore nature's "divinely superfluous beauty." The pantheist in Thoreau said that we should so live as to be ready to relinquish life at the end of the cycle, as the leaf releases its grip on the branch to fall to the compost of earth. But such relinquishment, even when desired, is difficult to achieve. Jeffers may admire and exalt the untroubled and undivided participation of wind and wave, of rock and hawk and buck in the physical and biological processes of nature, but he also knows that consciousness protects its winking flame, defers and defers its winking out.

Romantics have experienced nature — whether the pantheist Nature as God or the transcendentalist Nature as symbol of God — in two modes that they quite consistently distinguished as the beautiful and the sublime. (Immanuel Kant had formulated these conceptions for the Romantic generation, and Edmund Burke was particularly important in disseminating them for English-speaking nature-lovers.) The defining Romantic moment is the individual's encounter with nature, but nature is a Janus-face presenting the double countenance of the divine. The beautiful refers to landscape whose physical conformation and psychological affect welcomes, responds to, and nurtures the human. It is characterized by a modest scale that accommodates the human presence, regularity and symmetry of elements, smoothly curving lines, gentle gradations of height and depth, steady light and harmonious shades of color. The cooperative participation of the human transforms the beautiful into the pastoral: sun irradiating a fertile and cultivated landscape dotted with family farms, divine beneficence manifest in the reflections of the heavens above in the rivers and lakes below. Beautiful nature reveals the divine as the maternal ground, the source and sustenance and resting place of life.

By contrast, the physical conformation and psychological affect of the sublime landscape dwarfs the physical presence of the beholder so overwhelmingly that he or she feels psychologically reduced to the point of annihilation or absorption into the awesomeness of what he or she beholds. Characteristic features of the sublime include vastness of scale that suggests infinity, jagged and broken lines, extremes of soaring heights and dizzying declivities, intense contrasts of brightness and dark, the light either blinding or obscured by cloud over a harsh and dreadful landscape in which the irresistible energies of earth and wind, fire and water surge and collide. The sublime reveals the patriarchal visage of Yahweh behind and through the material cloud, and the human response is a volatile mixture of ecstasy and terror: exaltation at the limits of human endurance and comprehension, vision at the point of breakthrough and breakdown. The beholder at this pivotal and precipitous moment of epiphany is at once thrilled and threatened by the erasure of his frailty in the transcendental Other. He can go over the edge of the abyss — or pull back and seek the comfort and consolation of human company in his pastoral refuge. *Or* — and this is Jeffers' delicate and desperate balancing act — continue to test human limits against the sublime without going too far.

Jeffers conceived the sublime not in terms of a personal God but in terms of the impersonal forces of biological process. A reading of Jeffers' poetry, moreover, makes it immediately clear that he was drawn not to the comforts of the beautiful but to the risky revelations of the sublime, and indeed his poetry is his stratagem for pressing human limits without going too far. If the essential Calvinist situation is the confrontation between the individual and God, Jeffers the Calvinist pantheist elides that crux into the confrontation between consciousness and sublime nature, divinely inhuman, inhumanly divine. This is the drama of Jeffers' descriptive, lyric, and meditative poems, and its resolution can come only with crossing the barrier into silence. Jeffers speaks of "the beauty of things" often, but he really means the sublimity of things. He is the poet of the sublime without peer in American letters. He chose his place in the landscape and built Tor House not in some beautiful and sheltered valley among the protective hills but on the verge where the stone-strewn land drops to the expanse of the Pacific extending beyond the visible horizon. Tor House symbolizes both his engagement with and his shelter from the sublime landscape, and Hawk Tower symbolizes his concentering conjunction with Una in that engagement.

Some readers see Jeffers' inhumanist pantheism as resolving the dualism of mind and nature, subject and object in a pantheistic or ecological holism. In fact, however, the tragic exaltation of the poetry arises from the necessity and impossibility of resolving that dualism. Jeffers' Calvinist inhumanism makes his pantheism, in human terms, a divine tragedy, not a divine comedy. Even near the end, in "Carmel Point," he is still only able to say: "We must uncenter our minds from ourselves; / We must unhumanize our views a little." The telltale verb is "must"; not here or ever: "I *have* uncentered my mind from myself." Consciousness is indistinguishable from self, and vice versa. Language is the instrument and embodiment of consciousness; poetry is the voice of the human and can never be the voice of nature. Jeffers expresses in words the desire to "become confident / As the rock and ocean that we are made from." But we are not made from rock or ocean, and confidence or lack of confidence is a human experience, projected here onto rock and wave out of human need.

So this poetry, which again and again proclaims the end of the human and the totality of divine nature, turns on itself from time to time to recognize, in all honesty, the human dilemma, perhaps most acutely the poet's dilemma. His alien presence implicates him in the desecration of nature and renders his resort to language vain (both egoistic and futile). Consider, for example, these unsparing lines from "Margrave":

> I have humanized the ancient sea-sculptured cliff
> And the ocean's wreckage of rock
> Into a house and a tower,
> Hastening the sure decay of granite with my hammer,
> Its hard dust will make soft flesh;
> And have widened in my idleness
> The disastrous personality of life with poems. . . .
> (*Selected Poetry*, 389)

Jeffers knows that he can truly experience nature only by unknowing himself, but he also knows that he can therefore never know that experience because there will be no "he" to know nature. If language is a sign of his alienation, why speak? This is a devastating question that Jeffers poses to himself again and again. Can we "unhumanize our views" at least, in the words of the poem, "a little"? Can language be a sign and instantiation not just of disconnection but of connection? More precisely, can language in its disconnection thereby offer the frail human a protective stratagem for engaging the sublime without submitting to its annihilative totality? The poems answer, tentatively but persistently, yes. For example, the passage from "Margrave" reaches personal solace and poetic justification in a qualified assurance that is not without its own exculpatory pride:

> . . . I have projected my spirit
> Behind the superb sufficient forehead of nature
> To gift the inhuman God with this rankling consciousness.
> (389)

The violent sexual agon of *Cawdor*, centered on the triangle of Cawdor, Fera, and Hood, is punctuated by three deaths, blocking the narrative into three narrative movements like acts in a play, and these extraordinary descriptive cadenzas serve as something like the ruminative comment of a Greek chorus on the main action. The first is the slow and suffering death of old Martial, Fera's father, a lifelong failure hideously burned and blinded by the fire that brings them to Cawdor's door and brings Fera to Cawdor's marital bed. Jeffers describes his death biologically as the nerves disconnect and the brain cells decompose while "sparks of desire forty years quenched flame up fulfillment" in a last dream, quickly thwarted as "the altered cells become unfit to express / Any human or at all describable form of consciousness." The death of Hood occurs two thirds of the way through the narrative after an altercation with Cawdor on a precipice above the ranch. Father strikes son, and Hood slips over the edge and falls after a moment in which Cawdor hesitates to reach out to his son. Hood's young and strong body, the focus of Fera's lust, lies broken on the stones; the scattered brain cells that had felt "unitary" pulse briefly in the vain effort to reconnect until "the fragments of consciousness / Beginning to lapse out of the frailties of life / . . . enter another condition" and are extinguished in "the peace of the earth." These chillingly graphic descriptions of physical dissolution underscore the frailty of ego—consciousness and the indifference of biological process. For "the peace of earth" is not death, except for the individual, but, paradoxically and mysteriously, the totality of the "wild and shuddering" life in which even the seemingly inert stones on which Hood lies participate.

The death of the eagle at the end of the poem — justifiably one of the most famous and widely cited passages in Jeffers' work — presents another kind of participation in life and death. While men are "sieves of leaking desire," the poem instructs us, "the unsocial birds are a greater race." So much greater that Jeffers interrupts the climactic moment to wonder "How can I speak of you?" Nevertheless, human hubris or not, Jeffers presses limited human comprehension and language to the task of imagining what might be called the eagle's inhuman consciousness, free of ego and undivided from the biological processes of nature. The great bird, one wing broken years earlier by a bullet, has been kept in a cage and tended by Cawdor's daughter Michal. At last, her older brother George is permitted to put the eagle out of its misery with another bullet that fells its body, like the bodies of Martial and Hood, but mercifully releases his vital energy to return to its source in the sun. The several pages that follow the eagle's spirit spiraling up above the receding earth constitute one of the remarkable passages of the sublime in American writing, and its final lines provide the catharsis the poet seeks and the poem needs:

> Pouring itself on fulfillment the eagle's passion
> Left life behind and flew at the sun its father.

> The great unreal talons took peace for prey
> Exultantly, their death beyond death; stooped upward, and struck
> Peace like a white fawn in a dell of fire.

The violence here is not human destructiveness but the convulsions of continuity and renewal in which death and life, indistinguishable, constitute the divinity of nature.

The imagined, perhaps unrealizable ideal would therefore be, in the words of "Rock and Hawk," a fusion of the "fierce consciousness" and "bright power" of the hawk with the "final disinterestedness" and "dark peace" of stone. Nevertheless, Jeffers finds a flawed but honorable function for the activity of the conscious imagination in striving through language to exceed the limits of ego and thus achieve the disposition in which he can embody his experience in the poem with something of the sublimity of nature. In the words of "The Beauty of Things," "man, you might say, is nature dreaming"; and "to feel / Greatly, and understand greatly, and express greatly, the natural / Beauty, is the sole business of poetry." A late poem extends Lucretius' "De Reum Natura" ("On the Nature of Things") into "De Rerum Virtute" ("On the Virtue of Things") and thus offers an ethical and metaphysical validation of the linguistic mediation of / meditation on nature. The poem rehearses Darwinian evolution to the emergence of consciousness but now distinguishes between the neurotic impotence of ego-consciousness and the genuine, if limited, comprehension and articulation of divine beauty:

> The beauty of things means virtue and value in them.
> It is in the beholder's eye, not the world? Certainly.
> It is the human mind's translation of the transhuman
> Intrinsic glory. It means that the world is sound,
> Whatever the sick microbe does. But he too is part of it.

Jeffers' poetry, then, constitutes the effort — for his own sake and, he hopes, that of his shaken and converted readers — to stand apart from yet be a part of sublime Nature.

4

The poetic measure that Jeffers found for his act of translation is the long free-verse line. Whitman's exploration of such a line opened the way for modern poetry, and many readers and commentators, including Jeffers' disciple Everson, have made the connection between Whitman's line and Jeffers'. For his part, Jeffers insistently disclaimed Whitman's example and preferred to see the long verses of the Hebrew prophets and psalmists in the King James translation or the hexameters of Homer and Aeschylus as more kindred analogues and sources. It is easy to see that the democratic gregariousness and irrepressible hopefulness in Whitman's celebration of self and society would rankle with Jeffers, and the polar differences in their temperaments and outlook did inevitably give their long lines a different kind of weight and balance, a distinctive rhythmic movement and intensity and stress. Yet the polarity spans the expanse and bounds of the American experience: Whitman's "Starting from Paumanok" for his ebullient, swaggering journey down the seemingly open road finds its abrupt conclusion and somber counterpoint with Jeffers at "Continent's End."

In any case, the rhymed stanzas and blank verse of *Californians* broke open and gave way, from *Tamar* on, to a line without fixed or predictable length or movement. Some readers missed the tension of meter and complained that the lines could get too loose and flat. But Jeffers instinctively developed — out of the cadences of the Bible and the Greeks and, no doubt, Whitman — what he needed. His verse unit was a line large enough for the vast landscapes and tragically heroic characters of the poems; and yet it is flexible enough to play out or gather in its energies, as it accommodates, even within the same poem, the modulations between description, narrative action, lyric introspection, didactic statement, and apocalyptic vision.

Jeffers did not share the Modernist suspicion of rhetoric. Indeed, his goal was a rhetoric and measure that would enable and embody the encounter between the human and the inhuman. As the lines spill across the page and spill from one verse to the next, the poem takes form, playing out its violent dislocations while absorbing and assimilating them into the composure of the whole. The mayhem spawned of human will and human ego are steadily absorbed into the rhythms of wave and air, and the completed work assumes something of the finality and solidity of incisions on stone. What remains for us are the poems. Readers feel, beyond their shock and discomfort, the abiding power of the poetry because its language and form register both "the terrible intensity of Jeffers' religious passion" (Everson, vii) and the sublime monumentality of nature enclosing and quenching that terrible intensity.

Barth, Karl. *The Epistle to the Romans*, translated by Edwyn C. Hoskyns. New York: Oxford University Press, 1950.

Everson, William. "Introduction" to *Cawdor and Medea*. New York: New Directions, 1970.

Jeffers, Robinson. *The Selected Letters of Robinson Jeffers, 1897–1962*. Baltimore: The John Hopkins Press, 1968.

———. *The Selected Poetry of Robinson Jeffers*, edited by Tim Hunt. Stanford, Calif.: Stanford University Press, 2001.

Karman, James. *Robinson Jeffers: Poet of California*, revised edition. Brownsville, Ore.: Story Line Press, 1995.

Lynch, William F. *Christ and Apollo: The Dimensions of the Literary Imagination*. New York: Sheed and Ward, 1960.

Powell, Lawrence Clark. *Robinson Jeffers: The Man and His Work*. Pasadena, Calif.: San Pasqual Press, 1940.

Poetry

DIVINELY SUPERFLUOUS BEAUTY

The storm-dances of gulls, the barking game of seals,
Over and under the ocean . . .
Divinely superfluous beauty
Rules the games, presides over destinies, makes trees grow
And hills tower, waves fall.
The incredible beauty of joy
Stars with fire the joining of lips, O let our loves too
Be joined, there is not a maiden
Burns and thirsts for love
More than my blood for you, by the shore of seals while the wings
Weave like a web in the air
Divinely superfluous beauty.

THE EXCESSES OF GOD

Is it not by his high superfluousness we know
Our God? For to equal a need
Is natural, animal, mineral: but to fling
Rainbows over the rain
And beauty above the moon, and secret rainbows
On the domes of deep sea-shells,
And make the necessary embrace of breeding
Beautiful also as fire,
Not even the weeds to multiply without blossom
Nor the birds without music:
There is the great humaneness at the heart of things,
The extravagant kindness, the fountain
Humanity can understand, and would flow likewise
If power and desire were perch-mates.

TO THE STONE-CUTTERS

Stone-cutters fighting time with marble, you foredefeated
Challengers of oblivion
Eat cynical earnings, knowing rock splits, records fall down,
The square-limbed Roman letters
Scale in the thaws, wear in the rain. The poet as well
Builds his monument mockingly;
For man will be blotted out, the blithe earth die, the brave sun
Die blind and blacken to the heart:
Yet stones have stood for a thousand years, and pained thoughts found
The honey of peace in old poems.

TO THE HOUSE

I am heaping the bones of the old mother
To build us a hold against the host of the air;
Granite the blood-heat of her youth
Held molten in hot darkness against the heart
Hardened to temper under the feet
Of the ocean cavalry that are maned with snow
And march from the remotest west.
This is the primitive rock, here in the wet
Quarry under the shadow of waves
Whose hollows mouthed the dawn; little house each stone
Baptized from that abysmal font
The sea and the secret earth gave bonds to affirm you.

SALMON FISHING

The days shorten, the south blows wide for showers now,
The south wind shouts to the rivers,
The rivers open their mouths and the salt salmon
Race up into the freshet.
In Christmas month against the smoulder and menace
Of a long angry sundown,
Red ash of the dark solstice, you see the anglers,
Pitiful, cruel, primeval,
Like the priests of the people that built Stonehenge,
Dark silent forms, performing
Remote solemnities in the red shallows
Of the river's mouth at the year's turn,
Drawing landward their live bullion, the bloody mouths
And scales full of the sunset
Twitch on the rocks, no more to wander at will
The wild Pacific pasture nor wanton and spawning
Race up into fresh water.

NATURAL MUSIC

The old voice of the ocean, the bird-chatter of little rivers,
(Winter has given them gold for silver
To stain their water and bladed green for brown to line their banks)
From different throats intone one language.
So I believe if we were strong enough to listen without
Divisions of desire and terror
To the storm of the sick nations, the rage of the hunger-smitten cities,
Those voices also would be found
Clean as a child's; or like some girl's breathing who dances alone
By the ocean-shore, dreaming of lovers.

TO THE ROCK THAT WILL BE
A CORNERSTONE OF THE HOUSE

Old garden of grayish and ochre lichen,
How long a time since the brown people who have vanished from here
Built fires beside you and nestled by you
Out of the ranging sea-wind? A hundred years, two hundred,
You have been dissevered from humanity
And only known the stubble squirrels and the headland rabbits,
Or the long-fetlocked plowhorses
Breaking the hilltop in December, sea-gulls following,
Screaming in the black furrow; no one
Touched you with love, the gray hawk and the red hawk touched you
Where now my hand lies. So I have brought you
Wine and white milk and honey for the hundred years of famine
And the hundred cold ages of sea-wind.

I did not dream the taste of wine could bind with granite,
Nor honey and milk please you; but sweetly
They mingle down the storm-worn cracks among the mosses,
Interpenetrating the silent
Wing-prints of ancient weathers long at peace, and the older
Scars of primal fire, and the stone
Endurance that is waiting millions of years to carry
A corner of the house, this also destined.
Lend me the stone strength of the past and I will lend you
The wings of the future, for I have them.
How dear you will be to me when I too grow old, old comrade.

THE CYCLE

The clapping blackness of the wings of pointed cormorants, the great indolent planes
Of autumn pelicans nine or a dozen strung shorelong,
But chiefly the gulls, the cloud-calligraphers of windy spirals before a storm,
Cruise north and south over the sea-rocks and over
That bluish enormous opal; very lately these alone, these and the clouds
And westering lights of heaven, crossed it; but then
A hull with standing canvas crept about Point Lobos . . . now all day long the steamers
Smudge the opal's rim; often a seaplane troubles
The sea-wind with its throbbing heart. These will increase, the others diminish; and later
These will diminish; our Pacific have pastured
The Mediterranean torch and passed it west across the fountains of the morning;
And the following desolation that feeds on Crete
Feed here; the clapping blackness of the wings of pointed cormorants, the great sails
Of autumn pelicans, the gray sea-going gulls,
Alone will streak the enormous opal, the earth have peace like the broad water, our blood's
Unrest have doubled to Asia and be peopling
Europe again, or dropping colonies at the morning star: what moody traveller
Wanders back here, watches the sea-fowl circle
The old sea-granite and cemented granite with one regard, and greets my ghost,
One temper with the granite, bulking about here?

SHINE, PERISHING REPUBLIC

While this America settles in the mould of its vulgarity, heavily
  thickening to empire,
And protest, only a bubble in the molten mass, pops and sighs out, and the
  mass hardens,

I sadly smiling remember that the flower fades to make fruit, the fruit rots
  to make earth.
Out of the mother; and through the spring exultances, ripeness and
  decadence; and home to the mother.

You making haste haste on decay: not blameworthy; life is good, be it
  stubbornly long or suddenly
A mortal splendor: meteors are not needed less than mountains: shine,
  perishing republic.

But for my children, I would have them keep their distance from the
  thickening center; corruption
Never has been compulsory, when the cities lie at the monster's feet there
  are left the mountains.

And boys, be in nothing so moderate as in love of man, a clever servant,
  insufferable master.
There is the trap that catches noblest spirits, that caught — they say — God,
  when he walked on earth.

CONTINENT'S END

At the equinox when the earth was veiled in a late rain, wreathed with
    wet poppies, waiting spring,
The ocean swelled for a far storm and beat its boundary, the ground-swell
    shook the beds of granite.

I gazing at the boundaries of granite and spray, the established sea-marks,
    felt behind me
Mountain and plain, the immense breadth of the continent, before me the
    mass and doubled stretch of water.

I said: You yoke the Aleutian seal-rocks with the lava and coral sowings that
    flower the south,
Over your flood the life that sought the sunrise faces ours that has followed
    the evening star.

The long migrations meet across you and it is nothing to you, you have
    forgotten us, mother.
You were much younger when we crawled out of the womb and lay in the
    sun's eye on the tideline.

It was long and long ago; we have grown proud since then and you have
    grown bitter; life retains
Your mobile soft unquiet strength; and envies hardness, the insolent
    quietness of stone.

The tides are in our veins, we still mirror the stars, life is your child, but
    there is in me
Older and harder than life and more impartial, the eye that watched before
    there was an ocean.

That watched you fill your beds out of the condensation of thin vapor and
    watched you change them,
That saw you soft and violent wear your boundaries down, eat rock, shift
    places with the continents.

Mother, though my song's measure is like your surf-beat's ancient rhythm I
never learned it of you.
Before there was any water there were tides of fire, both our tones flow from
the older fountain.

POINT JOE

Point Joe has teeth and has torn ships; it has fierce and solitary beauty;
Walk there all day you shall see nothing that will not make part of a poem.

I saw the spars and planks of shipwreck on the rocks, and beyond the
  desolate
Sea-meadows rose the warped wind-bitten van of the pines, a fog-bank
  vaulted

Forest and all, the flat sea-meadows at that time of year were plated
Golden with the low flower called footsteps of the spring, millions of
  flowerets,

Whose light suffused upward into the fog flooded its vault, we wandered
Through a weird country where the light beat up from earthward, and was
  golden.

One other moved there, an old Chinaman gathering seaweed from the
  sea-rocks,
He brought it in his basket and spread it flat to dry on the edge of the
  meadow.

Permanent things are what is needful in a poem, things temporally
Of great dimension, things continually renewed or always present.

Grass that is made each year equals the mountains in her past and future;
Fashionable and momentary things we need not see nor speak of.

Man gleaning food between the solemn presences of land and ocean,
On shores where better men have shipwrecked, under fog and among
  flowers,

Equals the mountains in his past and future; that glow from the earth was
  only
A trick of nature's, one must forgive nature a thousand graceful subtleties.

POINT PINOS AND POINT LOBOS

I

A lighthouse and a graveyard and gaunt pines
Not old, no tree lives long here, where the northwind
Has forgot mercy. All night the light blinks north,
The Santa Cruz mountain redwoods hate its flashing,
The night of the huge western water takes it,
The long rays drown a little off shore, hopelessly
Attempting distance, hardly entering the ocean.
The lighthouse, and the gaunt boughs of the pines,
The carved gray stones, and the people of the graves.

They came following the sun, here even the sun is bitter,
A scant gray heartless light down wind, glitter and sorrow,
The northwind fog much kindlier. When shall these dead arise,
What day stand up from the earth among the broken pines?
A God rearisen will raise them up, this walking shadow?
Which tortured trunk will you choose, Lord, to be hewn to a cross?
I am not among the mockers Master, I am one of your lovers,
Ah weariest spirit in all the world, we all have rest
Being dead but you still strive, nearly two thousand years
You have wrestled for us against God, were you not conquered
At the first close, when the long horrible nails went home
Between the slender bones of the hands and feet, you frightfully
Heightened above man's stature saw the hateful crowd
Shift and sicken below, the sunburnt legionaries
Draw back out of the blood-drops . . . Far off the city
Slid on its hill, the eyes fainting. The earth was shaken
And the sun hid, you were not quieted. Men may never
Have seen you as they said in the inner room of the house,
Nor met you on the dusty suburb road toward Emmaus,
But nine years back you stood in the Alps and wept for Europe,
To-day pale ghost you walk among the tortured pines
Between the graves here and the sea.

                    Ah but look seaward,
For here where the land's charm dies love's chain falls loose, and the
    freedom of the eyes and the fervor of the spirit
Sea-hawks wander the huge gray water, alone in a nihilist simplicity, cleaner
    than the primal
Wings of the brooding of the dove on the waste of the waters beginning,
    perplexed with creation; but ours
Turned from creation, returned from the beauty of things to the beauty of
    nothing, to a nihilist simplicity,
Content with two elements, the wave and the cloud, and if one were not
    there then the other were lovelier to turn to,
And if neither . . . O shining of night, O eloquence of silence, the mother
    of the stars, the beauty beyond beauty,
The sea that the stars and the sea and the mountain bones of the earth and
    men's souls are the foam on, the opening
Of the womb of that ocean.

                    You have known this, you have known peace,
    and forsaken
Peace for pity, you have known the beauty beyond beauty
And the other shore of God. You will never again know them,
Except he slay you, the spirit at last, as more than once
The body, and root out love. Is it for this you wander
Tempting him through the thickets of the wolvish world?
O a last time in the last wrench of man made godlike
Shall God not rise, bitterly, the power behind power, the last star
That the stars hide, rise and reveal himself in anger —
Christ, in that moment when the hard loins of your ancient
Love and unconquerable will crack to lift up humanity
The last step heavenward — rise and slay, and you and our children
Suddenly stumble on peace? The oceans we shall have tamed then
Will dream between old rocks having no master, the earth
Forget corn, dreaming her own precious weeds and free
Forests, from the rivers upward; our tributary planets
Tamed like the earth, the morning star and the many-mooned
Three-belted giant, and those red sands of Mars between them,
Rust off the metal links of human conquest, the engines

Rust in the fields, and under that old sun's red waning
Nothing forever remember us.

                                    And you at peace then
Not walk by a lighthouse on a wild north foreland
Choosing which trunk of the poor wind-warped pines
Will hew to a cross, and your eye's envy searching
The happiness of these bleak burials. Unhappy brother
That high imagination mating mine
Has gazed deeper than graves: is it unendurable
To know that the huge season and wheel of things
Turns on itself forever, the new stars pass
And the old return and find out their old places,
And these gray dead infallibly shall arise
In the very flesh . . . But first the camel bells
Tinkle into Bethlehem, the men from the east
Gift you sweet-bedded between Mary's breasts,
And no one in the world has thought of Golgotha.

II

Gray granite ridges over swinging pits of sea, pink stone-crop spangles
Stick in the stone, the stiff plates of the cypress-boughs divide the sea's
    breath,
Hard green cutting soft gray . . . I know the uplands
And windy pastures where the great globes of the oaks are like green planets
Each in his place; I know the scents and resonances of desolate hills,
The wide-winged shadows of the vultures wandering across them; and I
    have visited
Deserts and many-colored rocks . . . mountains I know
From the Dent d'Oche in Savoy and that peak of the south past St. Gingolphe
To Grayback and Tahoma . . . as for sea-borderers
The caverned Norman cliffs north of the Seine's mouth, the Breton
    sea-heads, the Cornish
Horns of their west had known me as a child before I knew Point Dume or
    Pinos
Or Sur, the sea-light in his forehead: also I heard my masters
Speak of Pelorum head and the Attic rocks of Sunium, or that Nymphaean
Promontory under the holy mountain Athos, a warren of monks

Walls in with prayer-cells of old stone, perpetual incense and religion
Smoke from it up to him who is greater than they guess, through what
    huge emptiness
And chasms above the stars seeking out one who is here already, and neither
Ahunting nor asleep nor in love; and Actium and the Acroceraunian
And Chersonese abutments of Greek ridges on the tideless wave
They named, my spirit has visited . . . there is no place
Taken like this out of deep Asia for a marriage-token, this planted
Asiaward over the west water. Our race nor the great springs we draw from,
Not any race of Europe, nor the Syrian blood from south of Lebanon
Our fathers drank and mixed with ours, has known this place nor its like
    nor suffered
The air of its religion. The elder shapes and shows in extreme Asia,
Like remote mountains over immeasurable water, half seen, thought clouds,
Of God in the huge world from the Altai eagle-peaks and Mongol pastures
To the home of snow no wing inhabits, temples of height on earth,
    Gosainthan
And Gaurisankar north of Ganges, Nanda Devi a mast of the ship
We voyage upon among the stars; and the earth-sprung multitudes of India,
Where human bodies grow like weeds out of the earth, and life is nothing,
There is so much life, and like the people the divinities of the people
Swarm, and the vulgar worship; thence far east to the islands of this ocean
Our sun is buried in, theirs born of, to the noble slope of the lone peak
Over Suruga Bay, and the headlands of Hai-nan: God without name,
God without form, the Lord of Asia, is here as there.

                                                Serenely smiling
Face of the godlike man made God, who tore the web of human passions
As a yellow lion the antelope-hunter's net, and freeing himself made free
All who could follow, the tissue of new births and deaths dissolved away
    from him,
He reunited with the passionless light sky, not again to suffer
The shame of the low female gate, freed, never to be born again,
Whom Maha Maya bore in the river garden, the Himalayan barrier
    northward
Bounding the world: is it freedom, smile of the Buddha, surely freedom?
    For someone
Whispered into my ear when I was very young, some serpent whispered
That what has gone returns; what has been, is; what will be, was; the future

Is a farther past; our times he said fractions of arcs of the great circle;
And the wheel turns, nothing shall stop it nor destroy it, we are bound on
    the wheel,
We and the stars and seas, the mountains and the Buddha. Weary tidings
To cross the weary, bitter to bitter men: life's conqueror will not fear
Life; and to meditate again under the sacred tree, and again
Vanquish desire will be no evil.

                    The evening opens
Enormous wings out of the west, the sad red splendid light beats upward
These granite gorges, the wind-battered cypress trees blacken above them,
The divine image of my dream smiles his immortal peace, commanding
This old sea-garden, crumble of granite and old buttressed cypress trunks,
And the burnt place where that wild girl whose soul was fire died with her
    house.

III

I have spoken on sea-forelands with the lords of life, the men wisdom made
    Gods had nothing
So wise to tell me nor so sweet as the alternation of white sunlight and
    brown night,
The beautiful succession of the breeding springs, the enormous rhythm of
    the stars' deaths
And fierce renewals: O why were you rebellious, teachers of men, against
    the instinctive God,
One striving to overthrow his ordinances through love and the other
    crafty-eyed to escape them
Through patient wisdom: though you are wiser than all men you are
    foolisher than the running grass,
That fades in season and springs up in season, praising whom you blame.

                                    For the essence
    and the end
Of his labor is beauty, for goodness and evil are two things and still variant,
    but the quality of life as of death and of light
As of darkness is one, one beauty, the rhythm of that Wheel, and who can
    behold it is happy and will praise it to the people.

BIRDS

The fierce musical cries of a couple of sparrowhawks hunting on the
 headland,
Hovering and darting, their heads northwestward,
Prick like silver arrows shot through a curtain the noise of the ocean
Trampling its granite; their red backs gleam
Under my window around the stone corners; nothing gracefuller, nothing
Nimbler in the wind. Westward the wave-gleaners,
The old gray sea-going gulls are gathered together, the northwest wind
 wakening
Their wings to the wild spirals of the wind-dance.
Fresh as the air, salt as the foam, play birds in the bright wind, fly falcons
Forgetting the oak and the pinewood, come gulls
From the Carmel sands and the sands at the river-mouth, from Lobos and
 out of the limitless
Power of the mass of the sea, for a poem
Needs multitude, multitudes of thoughts, all fierce, all flesh-eaters,
 musically clamorous
Bright hawks that hover and dart headlong, and ungainly
Gray hungers fledged with desire of transgression, salt slimed beaks, from
 the sharp
Rock-shores of the world and the secret waters.

BOATS IN A FOG

Sports and gallantries, the stage, the arts, the antics of dancers,
The exuberant voices of music,
Have charm for children but lack nobility; it is bitter earnestness
That makes beauty; the mind
Knows, grown adult.

                       A sudden fog-drift muffled the ocean,
A throbbing of engines moved in it,
At length, a stone's throw out, between the rocks and the vapor,
One by one moved shadows
Out of the mystery, shadows, fishing-boats, trailing each other
Following the cliff for guidance,
Holding a difficult path between the peril of the sea-fog
And the foam on the shore granite.
One by one, trailing their leader, six crept by me,
Out of the vapor and into it,
The throb of their engines subdued by the fog, patient and cautious,
Coasting all round the peninsula
Back to the buoys in Monterey harbor. A flight of pelicans
Is nothing lovelier to look at;
The flight of the planets is nothing nobler; all the arts lose virtue
Against the essential reality
Of creatures going about their business among the equally
Earnest elements of nature.

GRANITE AND CYPRESS

White-maned, wide-throated, the heavy-shouldered children of the
    wind leap at the sea-cliff.
The invisible falcon
Brooded on water and bred them in wide waste places, in a bride-chamber
    wide to the stars' eyes
In the center of the ocean,
Where no prows pass nor island is lifted . . . the sea beyond Lobos is
    whitened with the falcon's
Passage, he is here now,
The sky is one cloud, his wing-feathers hiss in the white grass, my sapling
    cypresses writhing
In the fury of his passage
Dare not dream of their centuries of future endurance of tempest. (I have
    granite and cypress,
Both long-lasting,
Planted in the earth; but the granite sea-bowlders are prey to no hawk's
    wing, they have taken worse pounding,
Like me they remember
Old wars and are quiet; for we think that the future is one piece with the
    past, we wonder why tree-tops
And people are so shaken.)

PHENOMENA

Great-enough both accepts and subdues; the great frame takes all
   creatures;
From the greatness of their element they all take beauty.
Gulls; and the dingy freightship lurching south in the eye of a rain-wind;
The air-plane dipping over the hill; hawks hovering
The white grass of the headland; cormorants roosting upon the guano-
Whitened skerries; pelicans awind; sea-slime
Shining at night in the wave-stir like drowned men's lanterns; smugglers
   signaling
A cargo to land; or the old Point Pinos lighthouse
Lawfully winking over dark water; the flight of the twilight herons,
Lonely wings and a cry; or with motor-vibrations
That hum in the rock like a new storm-tone of the ocean's to turn eyes
   westward
The navy's new-bought Zeppelin going by in the twilight,
Far out seaward; relative only to the evening star and the ocean
It slides into a cloud over Point Lobos.

DOORS TO PEACE

Sphere beyond sphere
Of blazing crystal . . . .
I see the half moon rise at midday
Over the rocks in the air's clearness.
The spirit of the moon with blazing wings,
The arms uplifted, the eyes in ecstasy,
Stands on that crystal round, as the others
On the pale hills . . . and the ocean
Rounds like a dew-drop, the huge dome
Hangs inconceivably above,
The spirit spiring from it,
The arms uplifted, the eyes in ecstasy,
And though the sun's not to be borne
I see the spirit of the sun standing
On the unendurable dome of crystal,
Not looking down at his adorers,
The arms uplifted, the eyes in ecstasy
. . . Toward whom? Sphere beyond sphere,
Dome above dome the stars
Tower with winged figures
And the eyes of ecstasy . . .

I think they admire the silence
Outside the stars, what should light love
But that which having in itself
Enough, needs not to shine nor move?
Love, motion, light, and change, imply
Inward insufficiency;
God's other shore knows none; they die
And all the suns will die to see.

I think . . . I think says the brain . . .
But the little spire with the eyes of ecstasy
On the brain's dome is the life,
Not thinking anything,
But flaming . . . little fool you will cease
Flaming when you flame up to peace.

POST MORTEM

Happy people die whole, they are all dissolved in a moment, they have
  had what they wanted,
No hard gifts; the unhappy
Linger a space, but pain is a thing that is glad to be forgotten; but one who
  has given
His heart to a cause or a country,
His ghost may spaniel it a while, disconsolate to watch it. I was wondering
  how long the spirit
That sheds this verse will remain
When the nostrils are nipped, when the brain rots in its vault or bubbles in
  the violence of fire
To be ash in metal. I was thinking
Some stalks of the wood whose roots I married to the earth of this place
  will stand five centuries;
I held the roots in my hand,
The stems of the trees between two fingers: how many remote generations
  of women
Will drink joy from men's loins,
And dragged from between the thighs of what mothers will giggle at my
  ghost when it curses the axemen,
Gray impotent voice on the sea-wind,
When the last trunk falls? The women's abundance will have built roofs
  over all this foreland;
Will have buried the rock foundations
I laid here: the women's exuberance will canker and fail in its time and like
  clouds the houses
Unframe, the granite of the prime
Stand from the heaps: come storm and wash clean: the plaster is all run to
  the sea and the steel
All rusted; the foreland resumes
The form we loved when we saw it. Though one at the end of the age and
  far off from this place
Should meet my presence in a poem,
The ghost would not care but be here, long sunset shadow in the seams of
  the granite, and forgotten
The flesh, a spirit for the stone.

PELICANS

Four pelicans went over the house,
Sculled their worn oars over the courtyard: I saw that ungainliness
Magnifies the idea of strength.
A lifting gale of sea-gulls followed them; slim yachts of the element,
Natural growths of the sky, no wonder
Light wings to leave sea; but those grave weights toil, and are powerful,
And the wings torn with old storms remember
The cone that the oldest redwood dropped from, the tilting of continents,
The dinosaur's day, the lift of new sea-lines.
The omnisecular spirit keeps the old with the new also.
Nothing at all has suffered erasure.
There is life not of our time. He calls ungainly bodies
As beautiful as the grace of horses.
He is weary of nothing; he watches air-planes; he watches pelicans.

APOLOGY FOR BAD DREAMS

I

In the purple light, heavy with redwood, the slopes drop seaward,
Headlong convexities of forest, drawn in together to the steep ravine.
    Below, on the sea-cliff,
A lonely clearing; a little field of corn by the streamside; a roof under
    spared trees. Then the ocean
Like a great stone someone has cut to a sharp edge and polished to shining.
    Beyond it, the fountain
And furnace of incredible light flowing up from the sunk sun. In the little
    clearing a woman
Is punishing a horse; she had tied the halter to a sapling at the edge of the
    wood, but when the great whip
Clung to the flanks the creature kicked so hard she feared he would snap
    the halter; she called from the house
The young man her son; who fetched a chain tie-rope, they working together
Noosed the small rusty links round the horse's tongue
And tied him by the swollen tongue to the tree.
Seen from this height they are shrunk to insect size,
Out of all human relation. You cannot distinguish
The blood dripping from where the chain is fastened,
The beast shuddering; but the thrust neck and the legs
Far apart. You can see the whip fall on the flanks . . .
The gesture of the arm. You cannot see the face of the woman.
The enormous light beats up out of the west across the cloud-bars of the
    trade-wind. The ocean
Darkens, the high clouds brighten, the hills darken together. Unbridled and
    unbelievable beauty
Covers the evening world . . . not covers, grows apparent out of it, as Venus
    down there grows out
From the lit sky. What said the prophet? "I create good: and I create evil:
    I am the Lord."

II

This coast crying out for tragedy like all beautiful places,
(The quiet ones ask for quieter suffering: but here the granite cliff the gaunt
  cypresses crown
Demands what victim? The dykes of red lava and black what Titan? The
  hills like pointed flames
Beyond Soberanes, the terrible peaks of the bare hills under the sun, what
  immolation?)
This coast crying out for tragedy like all beautiful places: and like the
  passionate spirit of humanity
Pain for its bread: God's, many victims', the painful deaths, the horrible
  transfigurements: I said in my heart,
"Better invent than suffer: imagine victims
Lest your own flesh be chosen the agonist, or you
Martyr some creature to the beauty of the place." And I said,
"Burn sacrifices once a year to magic
Horror away from the house, this little house here
You have built over the ocean with your own hands
Beside the standing boulders: for what are we,
The beast that walks upright, with speaking lips
And little hair, to think we should always be fed,
Sheltered, intact, and self-controlled? We sooner more liable
Than the other animals. Pain and terror, the insanities of desire; not
  accidents but essential,
And crowd up from the core": I imagined victims for those wolves, I made
  them phantoms to follow,
They have hunted the phantoms and missed the house. It is not good to
  forget over what gulfs the spirit
Of the beauty of humanity, the petal of a lost flower blown seaward by the
  night-wind, floats to its quietness.

III

Boulders blunted like an old bear's teeth break up from the headland; below
  them
All the soil is thick with shells, the tide-rock feasts of a dead people.
Here the granite flanks are scarred with ancient fire, the ghosts of the tribe

Crouch in the nights beside the ghost of a fire, they try to remember the
    sunlight,
Light has died out of their skies. These have paid something for the future
Luck of the country, while we living keep old griefs in memory: though
    God's
Envy is not a likely fountain of ruin, to forget evils calls down
Sudden reminders from the cloud: remembered deaths be our redeemers;
Imagined victims our salvation: white as the half moon at midnight
Someone flamelike passed me, saying, "I am Tamar Cauldwell, I have my
    desire,"
Then the voice of the sea returned, when she had gone by, the stars to their
    towers.
. . . Beautiful country burn again, Point Pinos down to the Sur Rivers
Burn as before with bitter wonders, land and ocean and the Carmel water.

IV

He brays humanity in a mortar to bring the savor
From the bruised root: a man having bad dreams, who invents victims, is
    only the ape of that God.
He washes it out with tears and many waters, calcines it with fire in the red
    crucible,
Deforms it, makes it horrible to itself: the spirit flies out and stands naked,
    he sees the spirit,
He takes it in the naked ecstasy; it breaks in his hand, the atom is broken,
    the power that massed it
Cries to the power that moves the stars, "I have come home to myself,
    behold me.
I bruised myself in the flint mortar and burnt me
In the red shell, I tortured myself, I flew forth,
Stood naked of myself and broke me in fragments,
And here am I moving the stars that are me."
I have seen these ways of God: I know of no reason
For fire and change and torture and the old returnings.
He being sufficient might be still. I think they admit no reason; they are the
    ways of my love.

Unmeasured power, incredible passion, enormous craft: no thought
    apparent but burns darkly
Smothered with its own smoke in the human brain-vault: no thought
    outside: a certain measure in phenomena:
The fountains of the boiling stars, the flowers on the foreland, the
    ever-returning roses of dawn.

CREDO

My friend from Asia has powers and magic, he plucks a blue leaf from
    the young blue-gum
And gazing upon it, gathering and quieting
The God in his mind, creates an ocean more real than the ocean, the salt,
    the actual
Appalling presence, the power of the waters.
He believes that nothing is real except as we make it. I humbler have found
    in my blood
Bred west of Caucasus a harder mysticism.
Multitude stands in my mind but I think that the ocean in the bone vault is
    only
The bone vault's ocean: out there is the ocean's;
The water is the water, the cliff is the rock, come shocks and flashes of
    reality. The mind
Passes, the eye closes, the spirit is a passage;
The beauty of things was born before eyes and sufficient to itself; the
    heart-breaking beauty
Will remain when there is no heart to break for it.

HURT HAWKS

I

The broken pillar of the wing jags from the clotted shoulder,
The wing trails like a banner in defeat,
No more to use the sky forever but live with famine
And pain a few days: cat nor coyote
Will shorten the week of waiting for death, there is game without talons.
He stands under the oak-bush and waits
The lame feet of salvation; at night he remembers freedom
And flies in a dream, the dawns ruin it.
He is strong and pain is worse to the strong, incapacity is worse.
The curs of the day come and torment him
At distance, no one but death the redeemer will humble that head,
The intrepid readiness, the terrible eyes.
The wild God of the world is sometimes merciful to those
That ask mercy, not often to the arrogant.
You do not know him, you communal people, or you have forgotten him;
Intemperate and savage, the hawk remembers him;
Beautiful and wild, the hawks, and men that are dying, remember him.

II

I'd sooner, except the penalties, kill a man than a hawk; but the great redtail
Had nothing left but unable misery
From the bones too shattered for mending, the wing that trailed under his
    talons when he moved.
We had fed him six weeks, I gave him freedom,
He wandered over the foreland hill and returned in the evening, asking for
    death,
Not like a beggar, still eyed with the old
Implacable arrogance. I gave him the lead gift in the twilight. What fell was
    relaxed,
Owl-downy, soft feminine feathers; but what
Soared: the fierce rush: the night-herons by the flooded river cried fear at its
    rising
Before it was quite unsheathed from reality.

BIXBY'S LANDING

They burned lime on the hill and dropped it down here in an iron car
On a long cable; here the ships warped in
And took their loads from the engine, the water is deep to the cliff. The car
Hangs half way over in the gape of the gorge,
Stationed like a north star above the peaks of the redwoods, iron perch
For the little red hawks when they cease from hovering
When they've struck prey; the spider's fling of a cable rust-glued to the
    pulleys.
The laborers are gone, but what a good multitude
Is here in return: the rich-lichened rock, the rose-tipped stone-crop, the
    constant
Ocean's voices, the cloud-lighted space.
The kilns are cold on the hill but here in the rust of the broken boiler
Quick lizards lighten, and a rattle-snake flows
Down the cracked masonry, over the crumbled fire-brick. In the rotting
    timbers
And roofless platforms all the free companies
Of windy grasses have root and make seed; wild buckwheat blooms in the
    fat
Weather-slacked lime from the bursted barrels.
Two duckhawks darting in the sky of their cliff-hung nest are the voice of
    the headland.
Wine-hearted solitude, our mother the wilderness,
Men's failures are often as beautiful as men's triumphs, but your returnings
Are even more precious than your first presence.

TOR HOUSE

If you should look for this place after a handful of lifetimes:
Perhaps of my planted forest a few
May stand yet, dark-leaved Australians or the coast cypress, haggard
With storm-drift; but fire and the axe are devils.
Look for foundations of sea-worn granite, my fingers had the art
To make stone love stone, you will find some remnant.
But if you should look in your idleness after ten thousand years:
It is the granite knoll on the granite
And lava tongue in the midst of the bay, by the mouth of the Carmel
River-valley, these four will remain
In the change of names. You will know it by the wild sea-fragrance of wind
Though the ocean may have climbed or retired a little;
You will know it by the valley inland that our sun and our moon were born
    from
Before the poles changed; and Orion in December
Evenings was strung in the throat of the valley like a lamp-lighted bridge.
Come in the morning you will see white gulls
Weaving a dance over blue water, the wane of the moon
Their dance-companion, a ghost walking
By daylight, but wider and whiter than any bird in the world.
My ghost you needn't look for; it is probably
Here, but a dark one, deep in the granite, not dancing on wind
With the mad wings and the day moon.

NINTH ANNIVERSARY

Only a fortnight out of nine years has found me afield
From the ocean-cliff where I perched my house,
And long before that I lived in hearing of the long voice
And thunder of the shore: yet to this hour
I never look west but shaken with a joyful shock of astonishment,
By dark nor by day: there the most glorious
Creature on earth shines in the nights or glitters in the suns,
Or feels of its stone in the blind fog,
Or shakes its hair in the storms: I never wake in my bed
But surprised with pleasure to hear it speaking.
An east wind brings me the smell of the river, all the others carry
The sea-fragrances, the salt and the sea-wings.
— What, did my blood before me live inland always? — Admire
One's next neighbor after nine years?

CAWDOR

I

In nineteen-nine a fire swept our coast hills,
But not the canyons oceanward; Cawdor's ranges
And farm were safe. He had posted sentinels,
His son George and his man Jesus Acanna,
On two hills and they watched the fire all night
Stream toward Cachagua; the big-coned inland pines
Made pillars of white flame.

Cawdor at dawn
Stood by his door and saw in the bronze light
That leaked through towers of smoke windowed with sanguine
Reflections of the burning, two does and a fawn
Spring down the creek-bed stones of his ravine
Fleeing from their terror, and then a tawny mountain-lion
With no eyes for the deer. Next walked a lame
Gray horse, a girl led it, a broken old man,
His face bound with a dirty cloth, clung weakly
To the limping withers. Cawdor recognized him
Though he was faceless, old Martial, who had got a place
In the hills two years before, a feeble old man
Marked for misfortune; his stock, the first year, sickened
With lump-jaw; when a cow died in the creek
Martial had let her lie there. Then Cawdor had ridden
And cursed him, and Cawdor with his man Acanna
Roped the horns to draw the carcass out of the stream,
But when they drew, it burst.
Now Martial came, he and his daughter Fera,
For refuge, having saved from the fire nothing
But their own lives and the lame horse.

The old man
Reeled and was dumb with pain, but the girl asked
For Hood Cawdor, and Cawdor said "Not here.
He left last winter." Hood was his second son,

The hunter, with whom he had quarrelled. And Fera Martial:
"We've come," she pointed toward the smoke-towers, "from that.
You are Hood's father. You've the same drooping eyes, like a big animal's
That never needs look sideways. I'm sorry, you'll have to take us in. My
  father is burnt, he is blinded.
The fire was on us before we awoke. He tried to fetch a bridle out of the
  burning stable.
There was a drum of coal-oil against the wall exploded and blew fire over
  his face.
I dragged him out of the fire." He said "Bring him in." "It wasn't dark," she
  answered, "the oaks were like torches
And all the hill roared like a wave. He says we can go in, father, here is the
  door-step."
The old man groaned, lifting his hand to his face but not touching it, and
  hung back from the door.
"I wish to God you had left me at home." She said "Your home?" "To be a
  blackened log with the others
Lying quiet," he said, "in the burnt hollow under the hill, and not have any
  care and not come
Blind and crying to my enemy's place." He turned in her hands and said
  "Oh Fera, where is the sun?
Is it afternoon?" She stood and held him. "Dear, only dawn. I think it must
  have come up, it's hidden
In the hell of smoke." "Turn me that way before I go in,
To the good light that gave me so many days. I have failed, and failed, and
  failed. Now I'll go in
As men go into the grave, and not fail any more."

He was in fact passive from that time on,
Except the restlessness of pain in bed
While his face scarred and the eyes died in the dark.
After the pain was lulled he seemed content
With blindness, it made an end of labor.

                              Cawdor meanwhile
Would somehow have sent him up coast to Monterey
To find other charity; but the girl Fera
Coming ragged and courageous out of the fire

With cool gray eyes, had troubled his tough heart.
He'd not seen her before that dawn; and the image
Of the young haggard girl streaked with the dirt of the fire
And her skirt torn to bandage her father's face
Lived like a plant in his blood. He was fifty years old,
And mocked at himself; she was nineteen, she said.
But being a beggar really, under the burden
Of that blind man to care for, discounted youth;
And Cawdor, whatever the next ten years might bring him,
Felt no weight in the fifty. He had been stronger
From his youth up than other men, and still
The strength seemed to increase, the only changes
Toward age were harder lines in the shaven face
And fewer ferocities; the black passions of anger
That used to blind him sometimes had almost ceased.
Perhaps for lack of cause, now the few people
He dealt with knew him too well to cross him. And he'd security
And rough abundance to offer.

                    When Martial was able
Fera led him out-doors about the house
To feel the sun. He said it had no solidness
So near the ocean. "At home in the dear cup of the hills it used to come
    down
Like golden hammers, yet I'm content. Now it's dulled. Is there a cloud?"
    She answered, "Cypresses planted
Around the house, but the wind has broken them so . . . Sit on this bench by
    the door, here it beats golden."
He sat, and soon handled a thing beside him on the warm plank. "What's
    this thing on the bench,
Like a saucer with little holes?" "An old sea-shell," she answered, "an
    abalone's. They grow on the ocean-reef;
All this black soil's full of their shells, the Indians brought up." He said:
    "Fera: while we stay here
Will you do something to lengthen the life you saved? When's the new
    moon? Go down when the tides drain out
In the dark of the moon and at full moon, gather me mussels and abalones,
    I'll drink the broth

And eat the meat, it is full of salts and nourishment. The ancestors of our
    life came from the sea
And our blood craves it, it will bring me years of health." She answered
    "He wants us to go to-morrow." "Go, where?"
"That I can't tell. Is the sun pleasant?" "Oh, we can't go," he said, "you
    needn't be troubled. The sun
Is faint but pleasant. Now is that Cawdor passing?" "No. Concha Rosas,"
    she answered. "She helps the cook.
She helped me when you were sick."

                                   Fera with private thoughts
Watched the Indian-blooded woman about her work
Pass in the dooryard, and go after a moment,
Carrying a pan under her arm, to the halved cask
Against the lift of the hill, where water trickled
From a wood pipe; tall weeds and calla lilies
Grew in the mud by it; the dark fat woman
Sat on a stone among them, paring and washing
Whatever was in the pan; and Fera said carefully:
"She has a child with blue eyes and she is an Indian.
She and the boy had their rooms in the house
When we came here, but Mr. Cawdor has moved them
To the old adobe out-building where Acanna
Lives with his wife." Her father listened or not, and answered: "Fera,
Am I still in the sun?" "Oh? Yes." "It is faint," he said, "but pleasant.
    I suppose now you can see the ocean
With golden scales on the broad blue?" "No," she answered, "we face up
    the canyon, toward the dark redwoods."

Cawdor's daughter Michal came by,
A blue-eyed girl of fourteen, nearly as tall as Fera.
She had a trap in her hand, and a live ground-squirrel
Dangled from it by the crushed paws. Then Fera
Left her father a moment to go with Michal
To the eagle's cage, to watch the captive be fed.
Against a cypress, a wide wire-screened box; no perch in it
But a wood block, for the bird's wing was broken.

Hood Cawdor, Michal's brother, had shot it, the autumn
Before he went away, and Michal had kept it alive.

She laid the squirrel inside and opened the trap.
The girls, their arms lacing each other's shoulders,
Set their faces against the wire to watch
The great dark-feathered and square-shouldered prisoner
Move in his corner. One wide wing trailed through filth
Quickening a buzz of blow-flies; the fierce dark eyes
Had dropped their films, "He'll never be tame," Michal said sadly.
They watched the squirrel begin to drag its body
On the broken fore-paws. The indomitable eyes
Seemed never to have left the girls' faces but a grim hand
Came forward and gathered its prey under its talons.
They heard a whispering twitter continue
Below the hover of the dark plumes, until
The brown hackles of the neck bowed, the bleak head
Stooped over and stilled it.

                    Fera turned at a shadow
And saw Cawdor behind her, who said "One thing it's good for,
It makes Michal catch squirrels. Well, Fera, you're ready to go to-morrow?"
    "Let me go back to my father,"
She said, "I've left him alone too long. No, we're not ready." He followed
    her; Michal remained.
She touched her father's hand and spoke of the sun.
Old Martial lifted his cloth face, that he wore
To hide the scars; his voice dulled through the cloth:
"It is faint but very pleasant. I've been asleep."
She said "Mr. Cawdor's here." And Cawdor: "How are you. Now that he's
    better, Fera, little Romano
(That's Concha Rosas' boy) could take him walking in the afternoons and
    let you have a free time
To ride with Michal. If you could stay here. It's pitiful to see youth chained
    to helpless old age.
However, I have to drive to Monterey in the morning. I've put it off as long
    as I could,

And now he's able." She looked at Cawdor's face and his hands, and said
    "He means, father, that we
Must go to-morrow. I told you." Who sighed and answered, "That would
    be a long journey for nothing at all.
Are people more kind there? Wherever an old pitiful blind man goes
Someone will have to lead him and feed him and find him a bed. The world
    is not so made, Fera,
That he could starve. There *is* a God, but in human kindness." Cawdor said
    gravely: "Now's the other fool's turn
To speak: it makes me mad to have to spread out my foolishness.
I never had time to play with colored ribbons, I was brought up hard. I did a
    man's work at twelve
And bossed a gang at eighteen. That gets you nowhere. I learned that ruling
    poor men's hands is nothing,
Ruling men's money's a wedge in the world. But after I'd split it open a crack
    I looked in and saw
The trick inside it, the filthy nothing, the fooled and rotten faces of rich
    and successful men.
And the sons they have. Then I came down from the city.
I saw this place and I got it. I was what you call honest but I was hard; the
    little Mexican
Cried when I got it. A canyon full of redwoods and hills guaranteed not to
    contain gold.
I'd what I wanted, and have lived unshaken. My wife died when Michal was
    born; and I was sorry,
She seemed frightened at the end; but life was not changed.
I am fifty years old, the boys have grown up; and now I'm caught with
    wanting something and my life is changed.
I haven't slept for some nights. You'd think I might have been safe at fifty.
    Oh, I'm still my own master
And will not beg anything of you. Old blind man your girl's beautiful, I saw
    her come down the canyon
Like a fawn out of the fire. If she is willing: if you are willing, Fera, this
    place is yours.
It's no palace and no kingdom: but you are a beggar. It might be better for
    you to live
In a lonely place than lead your old blind-man up the cold street
And catch dimes in his hat. If you're not willing:

I'll tell you something. You are not safe here, by God you're not. I've been
    my own master;
But now I'm troubled with two wolves tearing each other: to kneel down
    like a fool and worship you,
And the other thing." She whitened and smiled. "I'm not afraid: but I'm not
    experienced. Marriage you mean?
There's no security in anything less. We are, as you say, beggars: we want
    security." Old Martial
Groped and muttered against her. She laughed: "I'm driving a bargain: be
    quiet father." Cawdor said sadly:
"I think that I am the one being made a fool of, old man, not you. Fera if
    you were willing
We'd drive up and be married to-morrow. And then . . . there must be
    something . . . clothes, clothes: you look ridiculous
Bursting through Michal's like the bud of a poppy." She stood quietly and
    looked over the dooryard
At Concha Rosas peeling potatoes beside the fountain. "Who's that
    wide-lapped dark o' the moon
Among the lilies?" He said, "Why: Concha. You know her." "Oh, Concha.
    And now you've moved her out of the house."
"Yes," he said angrily. And Fera laughing: "There is nothing under the sun
    worth loving but strength: and I
Had some but it's tired, and now I'm sick of it. I want you to be proud and
    hard with me; I'm not tame
If you ever soften. Oh, yes, to your offer. I'd a friend once that had fine
    dreams, she didn't look forward
Into her mist of moon on the roses — not Rosas — you remember Edith,
Father? — with half the heart that races me to meet to-morrow." Then
    Cawdor shuddered with hope of love;
His face relaxing began to look like an old man's. He stooped toward Fera,
    to fondle or kiss,
She drew herself back. "Not now. Oh, I'll be honest
And love you well." She took her father by the arm. "The sun's passed from
    the bench, father, come in.
I'll build a fire on the hearth if you want." And Cawdor: "That's it! You like
    horses, that's what I'll give you.
You liked mine but I'll buy you better; Morales has a pair of whites as
    beautiful as flowers.

We'll drive by there to-morrow. Like kittens they are." He followed her
   in-doors.

Blue kingfisher laughing laughing in the lit boughs
Over lonely water,
Is there no man not duped and therefore you are laughing?
No strength of a man
But falls on folly before it drops into dust?
Go wicked arrow down to the ocean
And learn of gulls: they laugh in the cloud, they lament also.
The man who'd not be seduced, not in hot youth,
By the angel of fools, million-worshipped success,
The self-included man, the self-armored,
And never beguiled as to a bull nor a horse,
Now in his cooled and craglike years
Has humbled himself to beg pleasure: even power was better.
Laugh kingfisher, laugh, that is their fashion.
Whoever has discerned the vanity of water will desire wind.

II

The night of Cawdor's marriage, his son
Hood Cawdor lay in the north on the open sand-beach
Of a long lake. He was alone; his friend in that country
Who hunted with him, had gone to the Indian camp.
Hood slept beside his fire and seemed to awake
And hear the faint ripple, and wind in far firs,
Then all at once a voice came from the south
As if it had flown mountains and wide valleys yet clearly heard
And like a dying man's, "Hood, Hood. My son." He saw
His father's face clearly a moment after
Distorted either with pain or approach of death.
But then the actual stars of the night came through it,
Like those of a winter evening, Orion rising,
Altair and Vega going west. When he remembered
It was early autumn, he knew it must be past midnight.
He laid a flare of twigs on the live coals

Before he lay down; eyes on the opposite shore
Would have seen the sharp stars in the black crystal
Of the lake cancelled by a red comet's tail.

That night and in the morning Hood had no doubt
His father had just died or approached death;
But dreams and visions are an obscure coinage
No sane person takes faithfully. He thought of writing
To his sister Michal; he had no habit of writing.
Months later, after the rains began and cramped
His migrant hunting, he thought not with much sorrow
Yet mournfully, of his father as dead; and thought
That he'd a share in the place unless he'd been,
As appeared likely, cut off by a written will.
No doubt it was too late to see the old man,
Yet he'd go south. He sold his horse and shot-gun, took his rifle and
    went south.

                              He approached home
Over the hills, not by the coast-road from Monterey. Miles beyond miles a
    fire had devoured
Until he looked from the height into the redwood canyons pitching to the
    ocean, these were unhurt,
Dark green and strong. Then he believed his father could not have died.

                                                                    The
    first canyon he entered
A mountain-lion stood stilted on a bare slope between alder and redwood
    watching him come down:
Like the owner of the place: he slid the rifle-stock to his cheek thinking
    "The hills have not been hunted
Since I've been gone"; he fired, and the lank August-pasture-colored body
    somersaulted
Over the ridge; he found it lying under a laurel-bush. The skinning was a
    long toil; Hood came
Burdened across the fall of twilight to the great dome of high-cliffed
    granite, they call it the Rock,
That stands out of the hill at the head of Cawdor's canyon.

                                                                    Here, after
    the trivial violent quarrel
That sped him from home the year before, he had built a fire at dusk hoping
    Michal would see it
And come to bid him good-bye; she had seen and come. He stood now and
    saw, down the great darkening gorge,
The reddish-yellow windows glimmer in his father's house, the iron-dark
    ocean a bank beyond,
Pricked at the gray edge with one pin-point ship's light. Deep, vast, and
    quiet and sad. After a little
He gathered sticks under the oaks and made a fire on the Rock's head,
    wishing Michal might see it.
If not, he could go down in the morning, (he'd blanket and food) and see
    whether the place was changed.

Michal had gone in-doors but Acanna saw it,
A bright high blood-drop under the lump-shaped moon,
When he was stamping stable-yard muck from his boots
Before he went in to supper. He said to the new farmhand
Dante Vitello, the Swiss whom Cawdor had brought
From Monterey: "You seen strangers go through?
Some fellow's got a fire on the Rock." Then Michal
Hurried her meal and went out. The fire waned,
Rayless red star up the blue-shadow-brimming
Moon-silver-lipped gorge. Michal went doubtfully
Up the dim moon-path by the lone redwood that lately
Excited by her father's marriage
She'd made a secret marriage with, and a law
That she must always touch it in passing. She touched it
Without much ceremony, and climbed, and peered
Under the oaks at the man out on the Rock's head.
Oh, it was Hood, in the red ember-glow. They met gladly;
The edge of shadow and moongleam down the gulf of the canyon crept up
    out of sight
Under the Rock before she went home. Hood said "You'll ask the old man
    whether he'd like to see me.
But tell him that I'll not stay. No plowing, I'm not a farmer." "You're still
    only a hunter" she answered.

By the house under the broken cypresses;
The saffron dawn from which Hood had descended
Still hung in the V of the canyon; Cawdor with morning friendliness, "Stay
    for a week if you like. Don't fear,
I won't set you at plowing, we've done the plowing. My wife's father," he
    said, "has your old room,
But you can have the one on the north, used to be Concha's." Fera Martial
    came out; she had changed
Amazingly from the sallow girl that Hood
Had seen two years ago at the lean farm. The eyes had not changed. A wind
    blew from her eyes
Like sea-wind from the gray sea. "Here's Hood," said Cawdor. "He looks
    more like you," she said, "than either of the others."
"As long as you don't ask him to work. George works, but this
Is only a hunter. Let him have the little north room for a week." Hood
    unstrapped the raw stiffening
Puma-skin from his pack. "I owe you a wedding-present," he said to Fera,
    "if you'll take this
I'll get it tanned. I shot it yesterday." Fera took in both hands the eight-foot
    trophy, she made
To draw it over her shoulders, "Stop. It's not dry, you'll stain your dress."
    "Who am I," she said impatiently,
"Not to be stained?" She assumed it like a garment, the head with the slits
    for eyes hung on her breast,
The moonstone claws dangling, the glazed red fleshy under-side
Turned at the borders, her bare forearm crossing it. "Sticky," she said and
    took it in-doors. "Come in."
He carried his pack, she led him up-stairs to the north room. "This was not
    yours when you used to live here."
"No. Mine was where your father is now." "Then who had this one?"
He answered "I don't remember: nobody: I guess it was empty." "That
    Rosas woman," she answered, "had it.
But the bed's aired." She left him there and went down.

He went out-doors to find Michal again
And couldn't find her; he wandered about and played with the horses,
Then Michal was coming up from the field seaward.
She carried a trap in her hand, and a live ground-squirrel

Dangled from it by the crushed paws, the white-rimmed
Eyes dull with pain, it had lain caught all night.
"What's that, Michal, why don't you kill it?" "A treat for the eagle.
I've taught him to eat beef but he loves to kill.
Oh squirrels are scarce in winter." "What, you've still got the eagle?"
"Yes. Come and watch."

               Hood remembered great sails
Coasting the hill and the redwoods. He'd shot for the breast,
But the bird's fate having captivity in it
Took in the wing-bone, against the shoulder, the messenger
Of human love; the broad oar of the wing broke upward
And stood like a halved fern-leaf on the white of the sky,
Then all fell wrecked. He had flung his coat over its head,
Still the white talon-scars pitted his forearm.

The cage was not in the old place. "Fera," she said,
"She made me move it because it smells. I can't
Scrape the wood clean." Michal had had it moved
To the only other level on the pitch of the hill;
The earth-bench a hundred feet above the house-roof,
An old oak's roots partly upheld; a faint
Steep path trailed up there. One side of the low leaning
Bole of the tree was the eagle's cage, on the other
A lichened picket-fence guarded two graves,
Two wooden head-boards. Cawdor's dead wife was laid here
Beside a child that had died; an older sister
Of Hood's and Michal's.

               They stood and watched
The dark square-shouldered prisoner, the great flight-feathers
Of the dragged wing were worn to quills and beetles
Crawled by the weaponed feet, yet the dark eyes
Remembered their pride. Hood said "You ought to kill him.
My God, nearly two years!" She answered nothing,
But when he looked at her face the long blue eyes
Winked and were brimmed. The grim hand took the squirrel,
It made a whispering twitter, the bleak head tore it,

And Michal said "George wanted to kill him too.
I can't let him be killed. And now, day after day
I have to be cruel to bring him a little happiness."
Hood laughed; they stood looking down on the house,
All roof and dormers from here, among the thirteen
Winter-battered cypresses planted about it.

III

The next day's noon Michal said, "Her old father
Believes that food from the sea keeps him alive.
The low tides at full moon we always go down."
When Fera came they took sacks for the catch
And brown iron blades to pry the shells from the rock.
They went to the waste of the ebb under the cliff,
Stone wilderness furred with dishevelled weed, but under each round
     black-shouldered stone universes
Of color and life, scarlet and green sea-lichens, violet and rose anemones,
     wave-purple urchins,
Red starfish, tentacle-rayed pomegranate-color sun-disks, shelled worms
     tuft-headed with astonishing
Flower-spray, pools of live crystal, quick eels plunged in the crevices . . .
     the three intrusive atoms of humanity
Went prying and thrusting; the sacks fattened with shell-vaulted meat.
     Then Fera said "Go out on the reef,
Michal, and when you've filled the sack with mussels call Hood to fetch it."
     "Why should I go? Let *him*."
"Go Michal, I need Hood to turn over the stones." When Michal was gone
And walked beyond hearing on the low reef, dim little remote figure
     between the blind flat ocean
And burning sky, Fera stood up and said suddenly: "Judge me, will you.
     Kindness is like . . .
The slime on my hands, I want judgment. We came out of the mountain fire
     beggared and blinded,
Nothing but a few singed rags and a lame horse
That has died since. Now you despise me because I gave myself to your
     father. Do then: I too

Hate myself now, we've learned he likes dark meat — that Rosas —
a rose-wreath of black flesh for his bride
Was not in the bargain. It leaves a taste." Hood steadied himself against the
wind of her eyes, and quietly:
"Be quiet, you are telling me things that don't concern me, true or not. I am
not one of the people that live
In this canyon." "You can be cold, I knew that, that's Cawdor. The others
have kindly mother in them.
Wax from the dead woman: but when I saw your face I knew it was the pure
rock. I loved him for that.
For I did love him, he is cold and strong. So when you judge me, write in the
book that she sold herself
For someone to take care of her blind father, but not without love. You had
better go out on the reef
And help Michal."

He went, and kneeling beside his sister to scrape the
stiff brown-bearded lives
From the sea face of the rock, over the swinging streaks of foam on the
water, "Michal" he said
"I wish you could get free of this place. We must think what we can do.
God knows I wouldn't want you
Like the girls in town, pecking against a shop-window." "What did she want
to tell you?" "Nothing at all.
Only to say she loves the old man. Michal, keep your mind clean, be like a
boy, don't love.
Women's minds are not clean, their mouths declare it, the shape of their
mouths. They want to belong to someone.
But what do I know? They are all alike to me as mussels." The sack was
filled; reluctance to return
Had kept him hewing at the thick bed of mussels, letting them slide on the
rock and drop in the water,
When he looked up Fera had come. "Why do you waste them?" she said.
"You're right, waste is the purpose
And value of . . . Look, I've something to waste." She extended her hand
toward him, palm downward, he saw bright blood
Trickle from the tips of the brown fingers and spot the rock. "You're hurt?"
"Oh, nothing. I turned a stone,

A barnacle cut me, you were so long coming I thought I could do without
  you. Well, have you judged me,
With Michal to help?" "Let me see the cut," he said angrily. She turned the
  gashed palm cup-shape upward
On purpose to let a small red pool gather. She heard his teeth grating, that
  pleased her. He said
"I can't see," then she flung it on the ocean. "But you're a hunter, you must
  have seen many a wild creature
Drain, and not paled a shade." He saw the white everted lips of the cut and
  suffered a pain
Like a stab, in a peculiar place. They walked
And were silent on the low reef; Hood carried the sea-lymph-streaming
  sack on his shoulder. Every third step
A cold and startling shadow was flung across them; the sun was on the
  horizon and the tide turning
The surf mounted, each wave at its height covered the sun. A river of gulls
  flowed away northward,
Long wings like scythes against the face of the wave, the heavy red light,
  the cold pulses of shadow,
The croaking voice of a heron fell from high rose and amber.

                                                            There were
    three sacks to bring up the cliff.
Hood sent his sister to fetch a horse to the cliffhead to carry them home,
  but Michal without an answer
Went home by herself, along the thread of gray fog
That ran up the great darkening gorge like the clue of a labyrinth. Hood,
  climbing, saw on the cliffhead, unreal
To eyes upward and sidelong, his head cramped by the load, like a lit pillar
  Fera alone
Waiting for him, flushed with the west in her face,
The purple hills at her knees and the full moon at her thigh, under her
  wounded hand new-risen.
He slid the sack on the grass and went down. His knees wavered under the
  second on the jags of rock,
Under the third he stumbled and fell on the cliffhead. They were not too
  heavy but he was tired. Then Fera

Lay down beside him, he laughed and stood up. "Where's Michal? I sent her
    to fetch a horse." And Fera shivering:
"I waited for you but Michal went on. My father says that life began in the
    ocean and crept
Like us, dripping sea-slime up the high cliff. He used to be a schoolmaster
    but mother left him,
She was much younger than he. Then he began to break himself on bad
    liquor. Our little farm
Was the last refuge. But he was no farmer. We had utterly failed
And fallen on hollow misery before the fire came. That sort of thing builds
    a wall against recklessness.
Nothing's worth risk; now I'll be mean and cautious all the rest of my life,
    grow mean and wrinkled
Sucking the greasy penny of security. For it's known beforehand, whatever I
    attempt bravely would fail.
That's in the blood. But see," she looked from the ocean sundown to the
    violet hills and the great moon,
"Because I choose to be safe all this grows hateful. What shall I do?" He
    said scornfully: "Like others,
Take what you dare and let the rest go." "That is no limit. I dare," she
    answered. He looked aside
At the dark presence of the ocean moving its foam secretly below the red
    west, and thought
"Well, what does she want?" "Nothing," she said as if she had heard him.
    "But I wish to God
I were the hunter." She went up to the house,
And there for days was silent as a sheathed knife,
Attending her sick father and ruling the housework
With bitter eyes. At night she endured Cawdor if he pleased
As this earth endures man.

                A morning when no one
Was in the house except her father in his room,
She stole to Hood's room on the north to fall
On the open bed and nuzzle the dented pillow
With a fire face; but then sweating with shame
Rose and fetched water for some menial service

About her father's body; he had caught cold
And was helplessly bedfast again.

                              Meanwhile Hood Cawdor
With hunting deer at waterheads before dawn,
Evening rides with Michal, lucky shots at coyotes
And vain lying-wait and spying of creekside pad-prints
For the great mountain-lion that killed a calf,
Contentedly used six days of his quick seven
And would have gone the eighth morning. But the sixth night
The farm-dogs yelled furious news of disaster,
So that Hood snatched up half his clothes and ran out
Barefoot; George came behind him; they saw nothing.
The dogs were silent, two of them came at call
Under the late moonrise cancelled with cloud,
But would not quest nor lead. Then the young men
Returned to bed. In the white of dawn they found
The dog that had not come in the night, the square-jawed
Fighter and best of the dogs, against the door
So opened with one stroke of an armed paw
That the purple entrails had come out, and lay
On the stone step, speckled with redwood needles.

That postponed Hood's departure, he was a hunter
And took the challenge. He found the fighting-spot,
Scratched earth and the dog's blood, but never the slayer.

IV

                                       A sudden rainstorm
Beat in from the north ocean up a blue heaven and spoiled his hunting. The
    northwest wind veered east,
The rain came harder, in heavy falls and electric pauses. Hood had come
    home, he sat with Michal
Playing checkers; Fera was up-stairs with her father.
The blind man had grown feebler; he had been in fact dying since the fire;
    but now two days he had eaten

Nothing, and his lungs clogged. Most of the daytime
And half the night Fera'd spent by his bedside. He had lain deeply absorbed
    in his own misery,
His blindness concentrating his mood, until the electric streams and hushes
    of the rain vexed him,
Toward evening he fell into feverish talk of trivial
Remembered things, little dead pleasures. Fera gave patient answers until
    he slept. She then
Left him and slept heavily beside her husband.

                                      The rain had ceased,
    Hood saw a star from his window
And thought if the rain ceased he might give over his hunting and go
    to-morrow. But out of doors
Was little promise of the rain ceasing; the east wind had slipped south,
    the earth lay expectant. The house
Wore an iron stub for some forgotten purpose
Fixed upward from the peak of the roof; to one passing out-doors at
    midnight the invisible metal
Would have shown a sphered flame, before the thunder began.

                                            Fera
    before the first thunderclap
Dreaming imagined herself the mountain-lion that had killed the dog; she
    hid in leaves and the hunter
Aimed at her body through a gap in the green. She waited the fire, rigid,
    and through closed lids
Saw lightning flare in the window, she heard the crash of the rifle. The
    enthralling dream so well interpreted
The flash and the noise that she was not awakened but slept to the second
    thunder. She rose then, and went
To her father's room for he'd be awakened. He was not awakened.
He snored in a new manner, puffing his cheeks. Impossible to wake him.
    She called Cawdor. In the morning
They sent Acanna, for form's sake, not hope's, to fetch a doctor. Hood
    offered to ride, Acanna was sent.
The torrents of rain prevented his return, and the doctor's coming, to the
    third day. But northward
He rode lightly, the storm behind him.

                                    The wind had shifted before
        dawn and grooved itself
A violent channel from east of south, the slant of the coast; the house-roof
        groaned, the planted cypresses
Flung broken boughs over the gables and all the lee slope of the gorge was
        carpeted green
With the new growth and little twigs of the redwoods. They bowed
        themselves at last, the redwoods, not shaken
By common storms, bowed themselves over; their voice and not the ocean's
        was the great throat of the gorge
That roared it full, taking all the storm's other
Noises like little fish in a net.

                                On the open pasture
The cattle began to drift, the wind broke fences.
But Cawdor, although unsure and thence in his times
Violent toward human nature, was never taken
Asleep by the acts of nature outside; he knew
His hills as if he had nerves under the grass,
What fence-lengths would blow down and toward what cover
The cattle would drift. He rode with George, and Hood
Rode after, thwart the current in the cracked oaks
To the open mercy of the hill. They felt the spray
And sharp wreckage of rain-clouds in the steel wind,
And saw the legs of the others' horses leaning
Like the legs of broken chairs on the domed rims
On the running sky.

                            In the house Fera
Sat by her father's bed still as a stone
And heard him breathe, that was the master-noise of the house
That caught the storm's noises and cries in a net,
And captured her mind; the ruling tenth of her mind
Caught in the tidal rhythm lay inert and breathing
Like the old man's body, the deep layers left unruled
Dividing life in a dream. She heard not the roof
Crying in the wind, nor on the window
The endless rattle of earth and pebbles blasted

From the hill above. For hours; and a broken cypress bough
Rose and tapped the strained glass, at a touch the pane
Exploded inward, glass flew like sparks, the fury of the wind
Entered like a wild beast. Nothing in the room
Remained unmoved except the old man on the bed.

Michal Cawdor had crawled up the hill four-foot
To weight her eagle's cage with heavier stones
Against the storm, and creeping back to the house
Heard the glass crash and saw the gapped window. She got up-stairs
And saw in the eddying and half blinded glimmer
Fera's face like an axe and the window blocked
With a high wardrobe that had hidden the wall
Between the two windows, a weight for men
To strain at, but Fera whose nerves found action before
Her mind found thought had wrestled it into service
Instead of screaming, the instant the crash snapped her deep trance. When
    Michal came Fera was drawing
The table against the wardrobe to hold it firm, her back and shoulders
    flowing into lines like fire
Between the axe face and the stretched arms: "Ah shut the door," she said
    panting, "did Hood go with them?
He hasn't *gone?*" "Who? Hood?" "Coo if you like: has he gone?" "He went
    with father," she answered trembling,
"To herd the cows . . ." "Why are your eyes like eggs then, for he'll come
    back, Michal?" She went to the bedside
And murmured "He hasn't moved, it hasn't hurt him." But Michal: "Did you
    want Hood?" "Want him? I wanted
Someone to stop the window. Who could bear life
If it refused the one thing you want? I've made a shutter to hold although it
    sings at the edges.
Yet he felt nothing. Michal, it doesn't storm for a sparrow's death. You and
    I, Michal, won't have
A stir like this to speed us away in our times. He is dying." Michal answered
    "Dante Vitello's
Roping the hay-stacks, I'll fetch him Fera?" "What could he do while the
    wind continues, more than I've done?
We can stand draughts. Oh Michal, a man's life and his soul

Have nothing in common. You never knew my father, he had eagle
    imaginations. This poor scarred face
For whose sake neither nature nor man have ever stepped from the path
    while he was living: his death
Breaks trees, they send a roaring chariot of storm to home him.
Hood wouldn't leave without his rifle," she said,
"He didn't take the rifle when he went up?"
"Why no, not in this wind."

                        In the afternoon the wind
Fell, and the spray in the wind waxed into rain.
The men came home, they boarded the broken window.
The rain increased all night. At dawn a high sea-bird,
If any had risen so high, watching the hoary light
Creep down to sea, under the cloud-streams, down
The many canyons the great sea-wall of coast
Is notched with like a murderer's gun-stock, would have seen
Each canyon's creek-mouth smoke its mud-brown torrent
Into the shoring gray; and as the light gained
Have seen the whole wall gleam with a glaze of water.

V

There was a little acre in Cawdor's canyon
Against the creek, used for a garden, because they could water it
In summer through a wood flume; but now the scour
Devoured it; and after Cawdor had ditched the barns
Against the shoreless flood running from the hill,
In the afternoon he turned to save this acre.
He drove piling to stay the embankment; Hood pointed
The beams, and Cawdor drove them with the great sledge-hammer,
Standing to his knees in the stream.

                        Then Fera Cawdor
Came down the bank without a cloak, her hair
Streaming the rain, and stood among the brown leafless
And lavender shoots of willow. "Oh come to the house, Hood."
She struck her hands together. "My father is conscious,

He wants to speak to Hood, wants Hood." Who wondering
Gave the axe to his brother and went up.

They came to the room off the
short hallway; he heard
Through the shut door before they reached it the old man's breathing: like
nothing he'd ever heard in his life:
Slime in a pit bubbling: but the machine rhythm, intense and faultless. She
entered ahead
And drew a cloth over the wrinkled eye-pits; the bald scars in the beard and
the open mouth
Were not covered. "Ah shut the door," she said, "against the wind on the
stairway." He came reluctantly
Into the dreadful rhythm of the room, and said "When was he conscious?
He is not now." And Fera:
"He is in a dream: but *I* am in a dream, between blackness and fire, my mind
is never gathered,
And all the years of thoughtful wonder and little choices are gone. He is on
the shore of what
Nobody knows: but *I* am on that shore. It is lonely. I was the one that
needed you. Does he feel anything?"
He thought, this breathing-machine? "Why no, Fera."
"It is only because I am cold," she said wringing her hands, violently
trembling, "the cold rain-water
Rains down from my hair.
I hated my loose mother but this old man was always gentle and good even
in drunkenness.
Lately I had true delight in doing things for him, the feeding, cleaning,
we'd travelled so far together,
So many faces of pain. But now he has flown away, where is it?" She
mastered her shuddering and said
"All that I loved is here dying: and now if you should ask me to I would
strike his face
While he lies dying." But he bewildered in the ice-colored wind of her eyes
stood foolish without an answer,
And heard her: "Do you understand?" He felt the wind tempered, it fell in
tears, he saw them running

By the racked mouth; she ceased then to be monstrous and became pitiful.
     Her power that had held him captive
Ceased also, and now he was meanly afraid of what she might do. He went
     through the house and found Michal,
And brought her up to the room. Then Fera lifted her face from the bed,
     and stood, and answered "Come Michal.
This is the place. Come and look down and despise us. Oh, we don't mind.
     You're kind: I am wicked perhaps
To think that he is repulsive as well as pitiful to you. You hunter with a rifle,
     one shot's
Mercy in the life: but the common hunter of the world uses too many;
     wounds and not kills, and drives you
Limping and bleeding, years after years,
Down to this pit. One hope after another cracked in his hands; the school
     he had; then the newspaper
He labored day and night to build up, over in the valley. His wife my
     shameful mother abandoned him.
He took whiskey for a friend, it turned a devil. He took the farm up here,
     hunted at last
To the mountain, and nothing grew, no rain fell, the cows died
Before the fire came. Then it took his eyes and now it is taking his life.
     Now it has taken
Me too, that had been faithful awhile. For I have to tell you, dear dear
     Michal, before he dies,
I love you — and Hood for your sake, Michal —
More than I do this poor old man. He lies abandoned." She stood above
     him, her thin wet clothing
In little folds glued to the flesh, like one of the girls in a Greek frieze, the air
     of their motion
Moulds lean in marble; Michal saw her through mist in the eyes and
     thought how lovely she was, and dimly
Heard her saying: "Do you not wish you were like this man, Hood? *I* wish
     I were like this man.
He has only one thing left to do. It is great and maybe dreadful to die, but
     nothing's easier.
He does it asleep. Perhaps we *are* like this man: we have only one thing left
     to do, Hood,

One burning thing under the sun. I love you so much, Michal, that you will
    surely forgive
Whatever it is. You'll know it is not done wickedly, but only from bitter
    need, from bitter need . . ."
She saw him frowning, and Michal's wonder, and cried quickly:
"You needn't pity him! For even in this deformity and shame of obscure
    death he is much more fortunate
Than any king of fat steers: under the bone, behind the burnt eyes
There have been lightnings you never dreamed of, despairs and exultations
    and hawk agonies of sight
That would have cindered your eyes before the fire came.
Now leave me with him. If I were able I would take him up, groaning to
    death, to the great Rock
Over your cramp cellar of a canyon, to flame his bitter soul away like a shot
    eagle
In the streaming sky. I talk foolishly. Michal you mustn't come back until he
    has died, death's dreadful.
You're still a child. Stay, Hood." But he would not.

                                   He heard in the
    evening
The new farmhand talking with Concha Rosas,
His Alp-Italian accent against her Spanish-
Indian like pebbles into thick water. "This country
You cannot trust, it never need any people.
My old country at home she is not so kind
But always she need people, she never kill all.
She is our mother, can't live without us. This one not care.
It make you fat and soon it cutting your neck."
Concha answered inaudibly, and the other: "You Indian.
Not either you. I have read, you come from Ah-sia.
You come from Ah-sia, us from Europa, no one from here.
Beautiful *matrigna* country, she care for Indian
No more nor white nor black, how have she help you?"
Their talk knotted itself on miscomprehension
Until *matrigna* shaped into *madrastra*.
"Beautiful stepmother country."

Hood ceased to hear them.
Why, so she was. He saw as if in a vision
The gray flame of her eyes like windows open
To a shining sky the north wind sweeps, and wind
And light strain from the windows. What wickedness in the fabric
Was driving her mad with binding her to old men?
He went to the door to look at the black sky.
He'd leave the house to-night but pity and the rain held him.
He heard the eaves gutter in their puddles and rush
Of rivulets washing the dark.

While he was there
She came from the stair and whispered: for they were alone
In the dark room, the others in the lamplit room
At the table: "If I were hurt in the hills,
Dying without help, you'd not sneak off and leave me.
Oh, nobody could do that. Pull the door to
On that black freedom. Perhaps my father will die
This drowning night, but can't you see that I am a prisoner
Until he does: the wrists tied, the ankles:
I can neither hold nor follow.
No, no, we have to let them take their time dying.
Why, even on Cawdor's, on your father's account
It would be wicked to call despair in here
Before it must come. I might do strangely
If I were driven. You'll promise. Put your hand here."
She caught it and held it under the small breast
Against the one dry thinness of cloth. She had changed then.
He felt it thudding. "I am being tortured you know."
He shook and said "Until he dies I'll not go.
Dear child, then you'll be quieter." "When you said *child*,
Your voice," she answered, "was as hard as your father's.
Hood, listen, all afternoon
I have been making a dream, you know my two white horses,
They are like twins, they mustn't be parted.
One for you, one for me, we rode together in the dream
Far off in the deep world, no one could find us.

We leaned and kissed . . ." He thrust her off, with violent fear,
And felt her throat sob in his hand, the hot slender
Reed of that voice of hers, the drumming arteries
Each side the reed flute. She went crouching and still
To the stair; he stood in the dark mourning his violence.

But she had gone up into the snoring rhythm
Neither day nor night changed. Cawdor had asked her
Whom she would have to watch with her all night,
"For you must sleep a little." She had chosen Concha
Rosas; and that was strange, he thought she had always
Hated Concha. He came at the end of evening
And brought the brown fat silent woman.

                       Then Fera
Looked up, not rising from the chair by the bed
And said with a difficult smile over the waves of noise:
"I was thinking of a thing that worried my father, in the old days. He made
    a bargain with a man
To pasture his horse, the horse died the first week. The man came asking
    pay for a year's pasture
For a dead horse. My father paid it at last, I wouldn't have paid it." "No,
    hardly," he answered. And Fera:
"The bargain ends when the man dies — when the horse dies." She looked
    at her dying father and said
Shuddering: "I'm sorry to keep you up all night, Concha; but you can sleep
    in your chair. He was always
A generous fool, he wasn't made for this world." Cawdor looked down at
    the bed through the dull noise
Like surf on a pebble shore, and said that he'd been out to look at the
    bridge; it was still standing.
The rain would break to-night, the doctor would come to-morrow. "That
    would be late, if there were hope,"
She answered, "no matter." "Dear child," he said hoarsely, "we all die."
    "Those that have blood in us. When you said *child*,
Your voice," she answered, "was as hard as a flint. We know that you and
    the Rock over the canyon

Will not die in our time. When they were little children
Were you ever kind?" "Am I not now?" "Oh, kind." She leaned sidewise and smoothed
The coverlet on the bed, but rather as a little hawk slips sidelong from its flapping vantage
In the eye of the wind to a new field. "But about blood in the stone veins, could Concha tell me?
Look, his face now Concha, pure rock: a flick and it shows. Oh," she said and stood up, "forgive me.
For I am half mad with watching him
Die like an old steer the butcher forgot. It makes me
Mad at your strength. He had none: but his mind had shining wings, they were soon broken."

　　　　　　When Cawdor went out
She said to Concha "It is growing cold. Wrap yourself in the blanket before you sleep in the chair."
When Concha nodded she went and shook her awake, by the fat shoulder. "Did Hood make love to anyone
In those old days? They're hot at sixteen." "He never. Oh no." "You didn't serve the father and the sons?
Whom did he love?" "Nobody. He love the deer.
He's only a boy and he go hunting." Fera whispered from the throat: "I wish to God, you brown slug,
That I had been you, to scrape the mud from his boots when he came in from hunting; or Ilaria Acanna
Cooking him little cakes in the oak-smoke, in the white dawns when the light shakes like water in a cup
And the hills are foam: for now who knows what will happen?
Oh sleep, cover your head with the blanket, nothing has changed."

She went about the room and rested in her chair.
The snoring rhythm took her mind captive again,
And in a snatch of sleep she dreamed that Michal
Had stolen her lion-skin, the one that Hood had given her,
And wore it in the hills and was shot for a lion.
Her dead body was found wrapped in the skin.
There was more, but this was remembered.

                                                    Perhaps the minds
That slept in the house were wrought to dreams of death
By knowledge of the old man's ebbing. Hood Cawdor
Dreamed also of a dead body; he seemed a child; at first
He dreamed it was his father lay dead in the house,
But afterwards his father held him by the hand
Without a break in the dream. They looked through a door
Into the room in which his mother lay dead.
There an old woman servant, who had now been gone
These many years, prepared his mother's body
For burial; she was washing the naked corpse.
Matrigna; madrastra. He awoke and lay in the dark
Gathering his adult mind, assuring himself
The dream grew from no memory; he remembered
His mother living, nothing of seeing her dead.
Yes, of the burial a little; the oak on the hill,
And the red earth. His thought of the grave calmed him
So that he was falling asleep.

                              But Fera remained awake
After her dream. How could one drive a wedge
Between the father and the son? There was not now
Any affection: but Hood was loyal: or afraid.
They had quarrelled the time before. The snatch of sleep
Had cleared her mind.

                              She heard the snoring rhythm
Surely a little slower and a little slower,
Then one of the old hands drew toward the breast.
The breathing failed; resumed, but waning to silence.
The throat clicked when a breath should have been drawn.
A maze of little wrinkles, that seemed to express
Surprised amusement, played from the hollow eye-pits
Into the beard.

VI

The window was black still.
No cock had cried, nor shiver of dawn troubled the air.
The stale lamp shone and smelled. Ah, what a silence.
She crossed the room and shook Concha. "Get up, Concha.
He has died. I was alone and have closed his mouth.
Now I'll go out." She thought in the hallway,
"Besides, I am greedy to be caught in Hood's room.
We can but die, what's that. Where did this come from?"
She whispered, staring at the candle she held
Without a memory of having found nor lighted it.
She opened Hood's door and shut it behind her.

                                        "He has died!"
No answer. Then Fera felt the tears in her eyes
Dried up with fear. "You haven't gone? Are you here Hood?"
She saw him lifting his face from the shadows like a sea-lion from the wave.
    "I dreaded
You'd slip away from here in my night. It is finished and I
Alone was by him, your father's flitch of dark meat snored in a corner. He
    has died. All the wild mind
And jagged attempts are sealed over." Her voice lifted and failed, he saw her
    sleep-walker face
Candle-lighted from below, the shadow of the chin covering the mouth and
    of the cheek-bones the eyes
To make it the mask of a strained ecstasy, strained fleshless almost. Herself
    was wondering what sacred fear
Restrained her, she'd meant to go touch, but here desire at the height burned
    crystal-separate. He said, staring:
"Have you called my father? I'll dress and come, what can I do?" "Do you
    think I will call," she said quietly,
"Cawdor?" She stopped and said: "Death is no terror, I have just left there.
    Is there anything possible to fear
And not take what we want, openly with both hands? I have been unhappy
    but that was foolish
For now I know that whatever bent this world around us, whether it was
    God or whether it was blind

Chance piled on chance as blind as my father,
Is perfectly good, we're given a dollar of life to gamble against a dollar's
worth of desire
And if we win we have both but losers lose nothing,
Oh, nothing, how are they worse off than my father, or a stone in the field?
Why, Hood, do you sleep naked?"
She asked him, seeing the candle's gleam on the arm and shoulder. "I
brought no night-clothes with me," he sullenly
Answered, "I didn't expect people at night. What do you want?" "Nothing.
Your breast's more smooth
Than rubbed marble, no hair like other men in the groove between the
muscles, it is like a girl's
Except the hardness and the flat strength. No, why do you cover it, why may
I not look down with my eyes?
I'd not hide mine. No doubt I'll soon die,
And happy if I could earn that marble to be my gravestone. You might cut
letters in it. I know
It never would bleed, it would cut hard. *Fera Martial* you'd carve, the letters of
a saved name,
Why should they fall like grains of sand and be lost forever
On the monstrous beach? But while I breathe I have to come back and beat
against it, that stone, for nothing,
Wave after wave, a broken-winged bird
Wave after wave beats to death on the cliff. Her blood in the foam. If I were
another man's wife
And not Cawdor's you'd pity me." "Being what you are," he answered: he rose
in the bed angrily, her eyes
Took hold like hands upon the beautiful bent shoulders plated from the
bone with visible power,
Long ridges lifting the smooth skin, the hunter slenderness and strength:
"being what you are you will gather
The shame back on your mind and kill it. We've not been made to touch
what we would loathe ourselves for
To the last drop." She said "What were you saying? Do you think I should
be shameless as a man making
Love to reluctance, the man to you for a woman, if I had time, if you were
not going to-morrow?

If I just had time, I'd use a woman's cunning manners, the cat patience and
	watchfulness: but shame
Dies on the precipice lip." "I hear them stirring in the house," he answered.
	"You lie, Hood. You hear nothing.
This little room on the north is separate and makes no sound, your father
	used to visit his thing here,
You children slept and heard nothing. You fear him of course. I can
	remember having feared something . . .
That's long ago. I forget what. Look at me once,
Stone eyes am I too horrible to look at? If I've no beauty at all, I have more
	than Concha had
When she was more fawn than sow, in her lean years, did your father avoid
	her? I must have done something
In ignorance, to make you hate me. If I could help it, would I come
Fresh from the death of the one life I have loved to make myself
Your fool and tell you I am shameless, if I could help it? Oh that's the
	misery: you look at me and see death,
I am dressed in death instead of a dress, I have drunk death for days, makes
	me repulsive enough,
No wonder, but you too Hood
Will drink it sometime for all your loathing, there are two of us here
Shall not escape.

                  Oh, but we shall though, if you are willing. There is one
	clean way. We'll not take anything
Of Cawdor's, I have two horses of my own. And you can feed us with the
	rifle. Only to ride beside you
Is all I want. But I would waken your soul and your eyes, I could teach you
	joy.

       I know that you love
Liberty, I'd never touch your liberty. Oh let me ride beside you a week, then
	you could leave me.
I'd be your . . . whatever you want, but you could have other women. That
	wouldn't kill me; but not to be with you
Is death in torture." Her hope died of his look. "I know we came from the
	fire only to fail,

Fail, fail, it's bred in the blood. But," she cried suddenly, "you lie when you
    look like that. The flesh of my body
Is nothing in my longing. What you think I want
Will be pure dust after hundreds of years and something from me be crying
    to something from you
High up in the air."

                        She heard the door open behind her, she turned on
    the door. Cawdor had come.
She cried "Have you waked at last? You sleep like logs, you and your son.
    He has died. I can wake nobody.
I banged your door, but this one was unlatched and when I knocked it flew
    open. Yet I can't wake him.
Is it decent to leave me alone with the sow Concha in the pit of sorrow?"
    His confused violent eyes
Moved and shunned hers and worked the room, with the ancient look of
    men spying for their own dishonor
As if it were a lost jewel. "How long ago did you knock? I have been awake."
    "What do I know
Of time? He has died." She watched him tremble, controlling with more
    violence the violence in him; and he said:
"I know he has died. I came from that room." Then Fera, knowing
That Hood looked like a boy caught in a crime but herself like innocence:
    "How did you dare to go in?
Oh yes, the dead never stand up. But how did you dare? You never once hid
    your contempt
While he was living. You came and cursed him because our cow died in the
    creek. Did he want it to die?
Then what have you done just now, spat in his face? I was not there, he lay
    at your mercy." She felt
Her knees failing, and a sharp languor
Melt through her body; she saw the candle-flame (she had set the candle on
    the little table) circling
In a short orbit, and Cawdor's face waver, strange heavy face with the
    drooping brows and confused eyes,
Said something heavily, unheard, and Fera answered: "Certainly I could have
    gone in and called you, but I

Was looking about the house for someone that loved him. You were one of
 the hunters that hunted him down.
I thought that Hood ... but no, did he care? I couldn't awake him. This
 flesh will harden, I'll be stone too
And not again go hot and wanting pity in a desert of stones. But you ...
 you ... that old blind man
Whom you despised, he lived in the house among you a hawk in a mole-hill.
 And now he's flown up. Oh, death
Is over life like heaven over deep hell." She saw Michal in the door.
 "You're here too, Michal?
My father has died. *You* loved him."

                                        She said in the hallway,
"Are you well, Michal? I'm not; but when I slept
A snatch of the early night I dreamed about you.
You wrapped yourself in the mountain-lion skin
That Hood gave me, and Jesus Acanna shot you for a lion."

VII

Cawdor remained behind in the room,
But Hood pretended to have been asleep and hardly
Awakened yet. Certainly he'd not betray
The flaming-minded girl his own simplicity
Imagined a little mad in her sorrow. He answered
Safe questions, but the more his intent was innocent
The more his looks tasted of guilt. And Cawdor:
"When are you going?" "To-day." "That's it? By God
You'll wait until the old blind man is buried.
What did she call you for,
Yesterday in the rain?" "She said her father
Was conscious, but when I came he was not conscious."
"Well, he's not now," he answered, his brows drooping
Between the dawn and the candle. Dawn had begun,
And Cawdor's face between the pale window
And the small flame was gray and yellow. "Get dressed," he said.
He turned to go, and turned back. "You were such friends
With that old man, you'll not go till he's buried."

He went and found Fera, in the room with the dead.
But seeing her bloodless face, and the great eyes
Vacant and gray, he grew somberly ashamed
Of having thought her passion was more than grief.
He had meant to charge Concha to watch her
While Hood remained in the house. He forgot that, he spoke
Tenderly, and persuaded Fera to leave
Concha to watch the dead, and herself rest
In her own room. Michal would sit beside her
All morning if she were lonely. "And Hood," he said,
Spying on her face even against his own will,
"Wanted to go to-day, I told him to wait.
Why did you call him, yesterday in the rain?"
"Yesterday?" "You came in the rain." "If that was yesterday:
Our nights have grown long. I think my father called him,
(My father was then alive) wishing to talk
Of the Klamath country. He too had travelled. He despised people
Who are toad-stools of one place." "Did they talk long?"
"I can't remember. You know: now he has died.
Now the long-laboring mind has come to a rest.
I am tired too. You don't think that the mind
Goes working on? That would be pitiful. He failed in everything.
After we fail our minds go working under the ground, digging, digging . . .
    we talk to someone,
The mind's not there but digging around its failure. That would be
    dreadful, if even while he lies dead
The painful mind's digging away . . ." Cawdor for pity
Of the paper-white face shrunk small at dawn
Forbore then, he folded his doubts like a man folding
A live coal in his hand.

                Fera returned
To her father's room; she said, "Concha, go down to breakfast. Michal,
Leave me alone for God's sake." Being left alone she knelt by the bed: "In
    that dim world, in that
Dim world, in that dim world, father? . . . there's nothing. *I* am between
    the teeth still but you are not troubled.
If only you could *feel* the salvation."

She was mistaken. Sleep and delirium
are full of dreams;
The locked-up coma had trailed its clue of dream across the crippled
passages; now death continued
Unbroken the delusions of the shadow before. If these had been relative to
any movement outside
They'd have grown slower as the life ebbed and stagnated as it ceased, but
the only measure of the dream's
Time was the dreamer, who geared in the same change could feel none; in
his private dream, out of the pulses
Of breath and blood, as every dreamer is out of the hour-notched arch of
the sky. The brain growing cold
The dream hung in suspense and no one knew that it did. Gently with
delicate mindless fingers
Decomposition began to pick and caress the unstable chemistry
Of the cells of the brain; Oh very gently, as the first weak breath of wind in
a wood: the storm is still far,
The leaves are stirred faintly to a gentle whispering: the nerve-cells, by what
would soon destroy them, were stirred
To a gentle whispering. Or one might say the brain began to glow, with its
own light, in the starless
Darkness under the dead bone sky; like bits of rotting wood on the floor of
the night forest
Warm rains have soaked, you see them beside the path shine like vague eyes.
So gently the dead man's brain
Glowing by itself made and enjoyed its dream.

The nights of many years
before this time
He had been dreaming the sweetness of death, as a starved man dreams
bread, but now decomposition
Reversed the chemistry; who had adored in sleep under so many disguises
the dark redeemer
In death across a thousand metaphors of form and action celebrated life.
Whatever he had wanted
To do or become was now accomplished, each bud that had been nipped
and fallen grew out to a branch,
Sparks of desire forty years quenched flamed up fulfilment.

Out of time, undistracted by the nudging pulse-beat, perfectly real to itself being insulated

From all touch of reality the dream triumphed, building from past experience present paradise

More intense as the decay quickened, but ever more primitive as it proceeded, until the ecstasy

Soared through a flighty carnival of wines and women to the simple delight of eating flesh, and tended

Even higher, to an unconditional delight. But then the interconnections between the groups of the brain

Failing, the dreamer and the dream split into multitude. Soon the altered cells became unfit to express

Any human or at all describable form of consciousness.

                                        Pain and pleasure
            are not to be thought
Important enough to require balancing: these flashes of post-mortal felicity by mindless decay

Played on the breaking harp by no means countervalued the excess of previous pain. Such discords

In the passionate terms of human experience are not resolved, nor worth it.

                                                    The
            ecstasy in its timelessness
Resembled the eternal heaven of the Christian myth, but actually the nerve-pulp as organ of pleasure

Was played to pieces in a few hours, before the day's end. Afterwards it entered importance again

Through worms and flesh-dissolving bacteria. The personal show was over, the mountain earnest continued

In the earth and air.

                But Fera in her false earnestness
Of passionate life knelt by the bed weeping.
She ceased when Michal returned. Later in the morning
She sent Michal to look for Hood and ask him
Whether he would surely stay as Cawdor had said
Until they buried her father. "Tell him to come

Himself and tell me." Michal came back: "He said
That he was not able to come; but he would stay."
At noon she saw him. She dressed and went to the table,
Where Cawdor sat and watched them. Hood shunned her eyes;
She too was silent.

                    In the afternoon Cawdor came up
And said "The doctor has come." "Why Michal," she said, "but that's a pity.
Came all the sloppy way for nothing, the doctor." "No," Cawdor said. "I
    want you to see him, Fera.
You are not well." She went and saw him, in her father's room, where
    Concha with some childhood-surviving
Belief in magic had set two ritual candles burning by the bed of death. The
    doctor hastily
Covered the face, the candle-flames went over in the wind of the cloth. Fera
    stood quietly and said
She had no illness, and her father was dead. "I'm sorry you've come so far
    for nothing." "Oh, well," he answered,
"The coast's beautiful after the rain. I'll have the drive." "Like this old man,"
    she said, "and the other
Millions that are born and die; come all the sloppy way for nothing and
    turn about and go back.
They have the drive." The young doctor stared; and Cawdor angrily
Wire-lipped like one who hides a living coal
In the clenched hand: "What more do you want?" "Oh," she answered,
"I'm not like that"; and went out.

                    After the doctor had gone
She vomited, and became so weak afterwards
That Michal must call Concha to help undress her.
After another spasm of sickness her dream
Was like a stone's; until Cawdor awakened her
In the night, coming to bed. She lay rigid
And saw the fiery cataracts of her mind
Pour all night long. Before the cock crew dawn
Sea-lions began barking and coughing far off
In the hollow ocean; but one screamed out like torture
And bubbled under the water. Then Fera rose

With thief motions. Cawdor awoke and feigned sleep.
She dressed in the dark and left the room, and Cawdor
Followed silently, the black blood in his throat
Stood like a knotted rope. She entered, however,
Her father's room.

                            She was not surprised, no one was there
And Concha's candles had died. She fingered the dark
To find her father, the body like a board, the sheeted face,
And sat beside the bed waiting for dawn.
Cawdor, returned to his room, left the door open
To hear the hallway; he dressed, and waiting for dawn
Now the first time knew clearly for what reason
He had made Hood stay: that he might watch and know them,
What they had . . . whether they had . . . but that was insane:
One of the vile fancies men suffer
When they are too old for their wives. She in her grief?
He had not the faculty common to slighter minds
Of seeing his own baseness with a smile. When Hood had passed
The creaking hallway and gone down-stairs, and the other
Not moved an inch, watching her quiet dead,
Cawdor was cured of the indulgence jealousy,
He'd not be a spy again.

                            But Fera had heard
Hood pass; she knew Cawdor was watching; she thought
That likely enough Hood had risen before dawn
To leave the canyon forever. She sat like a stone
Turning over the pages of death in her mind,
Deep water, sharp steel, poisons they keep in the stable
To wash the wounds of horses . . .

VIII

Hood coming in to breakfast from the fragrant light
Before sunrise, had set his rifle in the corner by the door.
George Cawdor left the table and going out-doors
Stopped at the door and took the rifle in his hands

Out of mere idleness. Hood sharply: "Mine. Put it down!"
He, nettled, carried it with him to the next room,
There opened the outer door and lined the sights
With a red lichen-fleck on a dead cypress-twig.
Hood came behind him and angrily touched his shoulder,
Reaching across his arm for the rifle; then George
Who had meant to tease him and give it back in a moment,
Remembered a grudge and fired. The sharp noise rang
Through the open house like a hammer-blow on a barrel.
Hood, in the shock of his anger, standing too near
To strike, struck with his elbow in the notch of the ribs,
His hands to the rifle. George groaned, yet half in sport still
Wrestled with him in the doorway.

                         Hood, not his mind,
But his mind's eye, the moment of his elbow striking
The muscle over the heart, remembered his dream of the night.
A dream he had often before suffered. (This came to his mind later, not
    now; later, when he thought
There is something within us knows our fates from the first, our ends from
    the very fountain; and we in our nights
May overhear its knowledge by accident, all to no purpose, it never warns us
    enough, it never
Cares to be understood, it has no benevolence but only knowledge.) He
    struggled in his dream's twilight
High on the dreadful verge of a cliff with one who hated him
And was more powerful; the man had pale-flaming gray eyes, it was the
    wind blowing from the eyes,
As a wind blew from Fera's, that forced him to the fall
Screaming, for in a dream one has no courage nor self-command but only
    effeminate emotions,
He hung screaming by a brittle laurel-bush
That starved in a crack of the rock. From that he had waked in terror. He
    had lain and thought, if Fera should come
But yet once more pleading for love, he would yield, he would do what she
    wanted . . . but soon that sea-lion shrieking
From the hollow ocean thoroughly awaked him, his mind stepped over the
    weakness, even rubbed it from memory.

What came to him now was only the earlier dream
Mixed with its rage of fear, so that he used
No temperance in the strife with his brother but struck
The next blow with his fist shortened to the mouth,
Felt lips on teeth. They swayed in the gape of the door,
Hood the aggressor but George the heavier, entwined like serpents,
The gray steel rifle-barrel between their bodies
Appeared a lance on which both struggled impaled.
For still they held it heedfully the muzzle outward
Against the sky through the door.

       Hood felt a hand
Close on his shoulder like the jaws of a horse
And force him apart from the other, he twisted himself
Without a mind and fought it without knowing whom
He fought with, then a power struck his loins and the hand
Snapped him over. He fell, yet with limbs gathered
Came up as he struck the floor, but even in the crouch
His mind returned. He saw his father, the old man
Still stronger than both his sons, darkening above him;
And George rigid against the wall, blue-faced
Beyond the light of the door; but in the light,
Behind Cawdor, Michal with pitiful eyes.
He said, "Give me the rifle." George, who still held it,
Sucked his cut lip and gave the rifle to Cawdor;
Then Hood rose and stood trembling.

       But Fera on the stair behind them:
She had heard the shot and come down half way: "What have you killed,"
  she said, "the mountain-lion? You snapping foxes
What meat will you take and be quiet a little? Better than you
Lies quiet up here." But why did her voice ring rather with joy than anger?
  "You deafen the ears of the dead.
Not one of you there is worthy to wash the dead man's body." She
  approached the foot of the stair; her face
Was white with joy. "Poor Hood, has he hurt you? I saw him pluck you off
  with two fingers a beetle from a bread-crumb.
It's lucky for them they'd taken your gun away from you." Cawdor said
  somberly, "What do you want here? The boys

Have played the fool, but you can be quiet." "And George," she answered,
   "his mouth is bleeding. What dreams have stirred you
To make you fight like weasels before the sun has got up? I am a woman by
   death left lonely
In a cage of weasels: but I'll have my will: quarrel your hearts out."
Then Cawdor turned to Hood and gave him the rifle,
And said to George: "I'm going to the hill with Hood
And mark a place for the grave. Get down some redwood
From the shop loft, the twelve-inch planks, when I come down
I'll scribe them for you. And sticks of two-by-four
To nail to at the chest corners." Fera cried "What a burial.
A weasel coffin-maker and another weasel
To dig the grave, a man buried by weasels."
Cawdor said heavily, "Come Hood." And Fera, "The gun too?
Be careful after the grave's dug, I wouldn't trust him."
He turned in the door: "By God I am very patient with you
For your trouble's sake, but the rope frays."

They had gone and Fera said "What would he do,
Beat me perhaps? He meant to threaten me, Michal?
The man is a little crazy do you think, Michal?"
She walked in the room undoing the dark braids of her hair.
"Why should he blame me for what I say? Blame God,
If there were any.
Your father is old enough to know that nobody
Since the world's birth ever said or did anything
Except from bitter need, except from bitter need. How old are you Michal?"
"Fifteen," she said. "Dear, please . . ." "Oh, you'll soon come to it.
I am better than you all, that is my sorrow.
What you think is not true." She returned up-stairs
To the still room where one window was blinded
But the other one ached with rose-white light from clouds,
And nothing breathed on the bed.

       But Michal hasted
And went up the hill to look to her caged eagle.
Hood and her father, she feared, would have to move
The cage, to make room for the grave.

She returned and heard
A soft roaring in the kitchen of the house.
"Why have you got the stove roaring, Ilaria?"
"She want hot water," Ilaria Acanna answered,
"She put the boilers over and open the drafts,
I pile in wood." Fera came down. "Not boiling, not yet?
Put in more oak. Oh, are you there Michal?
Common water is fair enough to bathe in
At common times, but now. Let's look out-of-doors.
I want it hot, there are certain stains. Come on.
We'll be back when it's hot." In the wind out-doors
She trembled and said "The world changes so fast,
Where shall we go, to the shore?" Passing the work-shop
Beside the stable they heard a rhythmic noise
Of two harsh notes alternate on a stroke of silence.
Fera stopped dizzily still, and after a moment:
"Although it sounded like my father's breathing,
The days before he died, I'm not fooled Michal.
A weasel," she said, "gnawing wood. Don't be afraid."
She entered. George lifted his dark eyes
From the saw-cut in the wine-colored redwood planks,
And Fera: "Oh, have you planed them too? That's kind.
The shavings are very fragrant.
How long will these planks last in their dark place
Before they rot and the earth fills them, ten years?"
"These never will rot." "Oh, that's a story. Not redwood even.
There's nothing under the sun but crumbles at last,
That's known and proved. . . . Where's the other weasel?" He looked
Morosely into her face and saw that her eyes
Gazed past him toward the skin of the mountain-lion
That Hood had given her. It was nailed wide and flat
In the gable-end, to dry, the flesh side outward,
Smeared with alum and salt. "Your brother weasel,"
She said, "Hood, Hood. The one that nibbled your lip.
How it is swollen." Not George but Michal answered
That Hood was up on the hill; "they had to move
My eagle's cage." Fera looked up at the lion-skin:
"I'll take that, George, that's mine." "Hm, the raw skin?"

"No matter," she said, "get it down. It's for my father.
What else have we got to give him? I'll wrap him in it
To lie like a Roman among the pale people.
. . . On your fine planks!" "You're more of a child than Michal,"
He said compassionately. "When you said *child*,
Your face," she answered, "softened I thought.
It's not like Hood's." He climbed up by the work-bench and drew the tacks,
She stood under him to take the skin, Michal beside her. The scene in the
    dim workshop gable-end
Wakes a sunk chord in the mind . . . the scene is a descent from the cross.
    The man clambering and drawing
The tyrannous nails from the pierced paws; the sorrowful women standing
    below to receive the relic,
Heavy-hanging spoil of the lonely hunter whom hunters
Rejoice to kill: . . . that Image-maker, its drift of metaphors.
George freed the skin, Fera raised hands to take it.
Her small hard pale-brown hands astonished him, so pale and alive,
Folding the tawny rawhide into a bundle.
"Where's Cawdor," she said, "your father: on the hill with Hood?"
He had gone up to Box Canyon with Dante Vitello,
Michal answered. And Fera: "Oh, but how hard it is.
Perhaps it could be oiled? It is like a board.
I'll take it to him." But Michal remained with George,
Tired of her restlessness, and afraid of her eyes.

Fera went up carrying the skin in her arms
And took it into the house. Ilaria Acanna
Came out to meet her. "Your water's boiling." "Well, let it stand."
She laid, in the still room up-stairs, the hard gift
Over her father's body. "Oh, that looks horrible,"
She cried shuddering and twitched it off. To hide it from sight
She forced it into the wardrobe against the wall,
The one she had moved to block the broken window
In the wild time of storm. She stood and whispered to herself,
And eyed the bed; then she returned out-doors,
And up the hill to the grave, in the oak's earth-bench
Above the house. The pit was waist-deep already,
And Hood was in the pit lifting the pick-axe

Between the mounds of wet red earth and cut roots.
Acanna leaned on a shovel above the pit-mouth.
For lack of room they had dug west of the oak;
The two old graves lay east. The eagle's cage
Was moved a few feet farther west; Hood labored
Between the cage and the oak. Jesus Acanna
From under the low cloud of the oak-boughs, his opaque eyes
And Indian silence watched Fera come up the hill,
But the eagle from the cage watched Hood labor; the one
With dark indifference, the other
With dark distrust, it had watched all the grave-digging.

Fera stood among the cut roots and said,
Lifting her hand to her face: "I was worn out yesterday
With not sleeping; forgive me for foolish words.
I came up here to tell you: for I suppose
You'll go away to-night or to-morrow morning.
Well, I am taught.
I wish that when you go you'd take for a gift
One of my white ponies, they'll have to bear being parted.
Good-bye. Live freely but not recklessly. The unhappy old man
For whom you are digging the hole, lost by that.
He never could learn that we have to live like people in a web of knives, we
      mustn't reach out our hands
Or we get them gashed." Hood gazing up from the grave: "I'm sorry. Yes,
      early in the morning." He glanced at Acanna
And said, "One thing I know, I shan't find loveliness in another canyon, like
      yours and Michal's." She turned
Away, saying "That's no help," and seemed about to go down; but again
      turning: "I meant to gather
Some branches of mountain laurel. There are no flowers
This time of year. But I have no knife. It shouldn't be all like a dog's burial."
      "I'll cut some for you."
He climbed out of the grave and said to Acanna: "I'll soon be back. If you
      strike rock at this end,
Level off the floor." Fera pointed with her hand trembling: "The tree's in
      the gap behind the oak-trees.

It's farther but the leaves are much fresher. Indeed he deserves laurel, his
    mind had wings and magnificence
One dash of common cunning would have made famous. And died a cow's
    death. You and I, if we can bear
The knocks and abominations of fortune for fifty years yet, have as much to
    hope for. Don't come. I'm not
A cheerful companion. Lend me the knife."
He thought she had better not be trusted alone with it,
The mind she was in,
And went beside her, above the older graves,
He felt his knees trembling. Across the steep slope
To the far oaks. Dark aboriginal eyes,
The Indian's and the coast-range eagle's, like eyes
Of this dark earth watching our alien blood
Pass and perform its vanities, watched them to the far oaks.
But after the oaks had hidden them Acanna
Covetously examined the hunter's rifle
Left behind, leaning against the lichened fence
Of the older graves. It was very desirable. He sighed
And set it back in its place.

               Fera in the lonely
Oak-shielded shadow under the polished laurel-leaves: "Before you came
I used to come here," she caught her quivering under lip with the teeth to
    keep it quiet, "for solitude.
Here I was sure no one would come, not even the deer, not a bird; safer than
    a locked room.
Those days I had no traitor in my own heart, and would gather my spirit
    here
To endure old men.

               That I have to die
Is nothing important: though it's been pitied sometimes when people are
    young: but to die in hell. I've lived
Some days of it; it burns; how I'd have laughed
Last year to think of anyone taken captive by love. A girl imagines all sorts
    of things

When she lives lonely but this was never . . . Who knows what the dead feel,
    and it is frightful to think
That after I have gone down and stilled myself in the hissing ocean: roll, roll
    on the weed: this hunger
Might not be stilled, this fire nor this thirst . . .
For how can anyone be sure that death is a sleep? I've never found the little
    garden-flower temperance
In the forest of the acts of God . . . Oh no, all's forever there, all wild and
    monstrous
Outside the garden: long after the white body beats to bone on the rock-
    teeth the unfed spirit
Will go screaming with pain along the flash of the foam, gnawing for its
    famine a wrist of shadow,
Torture by the sea, screaming your name. I know these things. I am not one
    of the careful spirits
That trot a mile and then stand."

                                    He had bared his knife-blade to cut the
    bough, enduring her voice, but Fera
Caught the raised wrist. "Let it be. We have no right. The trees are decent,
    but we! A redwood cut
To make the coffin, an oak's roots for the grave: some day the coast will lose
    patience and dip
And be clean. Ah. Is it men you love?
You are girl-hearted, that makes you ice to me? What do you love? What
    horror of emptiness
Is in you to make you love nothing? Or only the deer and the wild feet of
    the mountain and follow them
As men do women. Yet you could dip that little knife-blade in me for
    pleasure, I'd not cry out
More than a shot deer, but I will never leave you
Until you quiet me." She saw that his face was gray and strained as a spent
    runner's beaten at the goal.
"Will you kiss me, once, you are going away in a moment forever? What do
    you owe Cawdor, what price
Of kindness bought you? This morning it was: he struck you and flung you
    on the ground: you liked that?" He gathered his strength

And turned himself to be gone. She caught him and clung,
And fallen to her knees when he moved outward, "I swear by God," she said,
    "I will tell him that you have taken me
Against my will, if you go from here before I have spoken. You'll not be
    hurt, Hood, you'll be far off,
And what he can do to *me* is no matter." He said "You have gone mad.
    Stand up. I will listen." But she
Feeling at last for the first time some shadow of a power
To hold and move him would not speak nor stand up, but crouched at his
    feet to enjoy it. At length she lifted
Wide staring eyes and fever-stained face. "I am very happy. I don't know
    what has told me: some movement
Or quietness of yours." She embraced his thighs, kneeling before him, he
    felt her breasts against them, her head
Nuzzling his body, he felt with his hand the fire of her throat, "Nothing,"
    he said
"Is worse nor more vile than what we are doing." "What? With a little . . .
    sin if you call it . . . kill a great misery?
No one," she thought, "ever tastes triumph
Until the mouth is rinsed with despair." She sobbed "I have found you."
    But when he had dropped the knife at the tree's root
To free his hand, and lay by her side on the drifted fall of the crisp
    oak-leaves and curled brown laurel-leaves,
Then she who had wooed began to resist him, to lengthen pleasure. "I have
    lighted the fire, let me warm my hands at it
Before we are burned." The face of her exultation was hateful to him. He
    thought of the knife in the leaves
And caught it toward him and struck the point of the blade into the muscle
    of his thigh. He felt no pain
A moment, and then a lightning of pain, and in the lit clearance: "I am not
    your dog yet," he said easily,
"I am not your thing." He felt her body shudder and turn stone above him.
    "What have you done?" "A half inch
Into the blood," he answered, "I am better." He stood up. "You will be
    grateful
To-morrow, for now we can live and not be ashamed. What sort of life
    would have been left us?" "No life

Is left us," she said from a loose throat.
"This mountain is dry." She stood and whispered "I won't do anything
    mean or troublesome. I pitied my father's
Failures from the heart, but then quietness came." Her teeth chattered
    together, she said "I will now go down
If you will let me?" He followed, limping from the Attis-gesture,
Outside the oaks and watched her creep toward the house.
The blood gliding by his knee he rubbed a handful of earth
Against the stain in the cloth to embrown the color,
And went faintly to the work he had left.

IX

                            Michal
Came up after a time with meat for the eagle.
While she fed it they had sunk the grave though shallow
To the hard rock and ceased. "Have you seen Fera
Lately?" Hood asked, "she was here wanting some greens
Because there are no flowers, but seemed to be taken sick
With grief and went down." "No. I was into the house
But not up-stairs." "We'd better see how she is.
Bring down the axe and pick-axe," he said to Acanna,
"But leave the spades." He stepped short, to conceal
His lameness. Michal asked him "What's the long stain?"
"Sap from the oak-roots, they're full of water."

                            They looked for Fera
All over the house and found her lying on the floor
The far side of her father's bed. Hood watched in terror
While Michal touched; he thought she had killed herself.
He had held an obscure panic by force a prisoner
All day but now it was worse, it was a wish to be gone,
"There's nothing I wouldn't give to have gone yesterday.
Oh pitiful child." She moved; she was not self-slain. She rose
To Michal's tugging hands and was led to bed
In her own room, hanging back but in silence.
Toward evening she dressed herself with Concha helping

In the blue serge that was the darkest she had
And went with the others up the hill to the burial.

A man at each corner carried the oblong box,
Cawdor and his sons and Dante Vitello. But Hood was lame
And when his left foot slipped on a stone his right
Failed with the weight. The stiff unseasonable
Calla lilies that Michal had found by water
Fell down the tilted lid; she gathered them up,
And when the box was lowered into its place
Dropped them upon it. Jesus Acanna had brought
The cords to use for lowering. All was done awkwardly
By shame-faced people, and the eagle watched from the cage.
The coffin grounding like a shored boat, the daughter
Of the tired passenger sighed, she leaned in the blindness
Of sand-gray eyes behind Michal toward Hood.
Her hand touched his, he trembled and stepped aside
Beyond Concha Rosas. Then Fera pressed her knuckles to her mouth
And went down the hill; the others remained.

Because of the dug earth heaped at the oak's foot
They were all standing on the west side the grave
Or at either end, a curious group, Cawdor's gray head the tallest,
Nine, to count Concha's child,
Intent, ill at ease, like bewildered cattle nosing one fallen. Not one of them,
    now that Fera was gone,
Had any more than generic relation to the dead; they were merely man
    contemplating man's end,
Feeling some want of ceremony.

                              The sky had been overcast; between the
    ocean and the cloud
Was an inch slit, through which the sun broke suddenly at setting, only a
    fraction of his passing face,
But shone up the hill from the low sea's rim a reddening fire from a pit.
    The shadows of the still people
Lay like a bundle of rods, over the shallow grave, up the red mound of
    earth, and upward

The mass of the oak; beyond them another shadow,
Broad, startling and rectilinear, was laid from the eagle's cage; nine slender
    human shadows and one
Of another nature.

                    Jesus Acanna
Saw something like a jewel gleam in the rays
On the heap of surface earth at his feet; he stooped
And picked it up; a knife-edged flake of wrought
Chalcedony, the smooth fracture was pleasant to feel.
He stood and fondled it with his fingers, not mindful
That his own people had chipped it out and used it
To scrape a hide in their dawn or meat from a shell.

Then Cawdor made a clearing noise in his throat
And said in heavy embarrassment: "We know nothing of God, but we in
    our turn shall discover death.
It might be good to stand quietly a moment, before we fill in the dirt, and so
    if anyone
Is used to praying" — he looked at Concha and Ilaria — "might say it in their
    minds." They stood with their eyes lowered,
And Cawdor took up a shovel and said impatiently
"Let us fill in." The sun was gone under the wine-colored ocean, then the
    deep west fountained
Unanticipated magnificences of soaring rose and heavy purple, atmospheres
    of flame-shot
Color played like a mountain surf, over the abrupt coast, up the austere
    hills,
On the women talking, on the men's bent forms filling the grave, on the
    oak, on the eagle's prison, one glory
Without significance pervaded the world.

                                Fera had gone down
To the emptied room in the vacant house to do
What she had imagined in the afternoon. In the pain of her mind
Nothing appeared fantastic; she had thought of a way
To trick death from the hands that refused life.
From Hood's own hands. She'd not be forgotten. She drew

The mountain-lion skin from where it was crumpled away,
And clothed herself in it, the narrow shoulders
Over her shoulders, the head over her head.
She bound it with bits of string and smoothed the wrinkles.
It would fool a hunter in the twilight; only her face
Must be turned from him. She fled from the house and hid
In the oaks against the hill, not far from the door.
The rosy light had waned from the cloud, wilderness-hearted
Twilight was here, embrowning the leaves and earth.
Concha and Ilaria and Concha's child came talking
And entered the house; kitchen windows were lighted.
The others delayed. Blue smoke began to veil out
And be fragrant among the leaves. She crouched in the oak-bush,
As every evening the wild lives of the mountain
Come down and lie watching by lonely houses.

Hood, when they took the redwood box to the house,
Had left his rifle in the stable, he came with Michal,
Having fetched it. They walked mournfully together,
For this was their last evening, he'd leave at dawn
For the free north. But nothing remained to say;
And through their silence, drawing near the house-door, Michal
Heard the stiff oak-leaves move, she looked and perceived
A life among them, laying her hand on his arm
She pointed with the other hand. The head and slant shoulder
And half the side unsheathed themselves from the oak,
The hindquarters were hidden. The long beast lifted
On straightened forelegs and stood quartering away,
The head raised, turned up the canyon. Hood held his fire,
Astonished at it, wasn't it one of the dogs?
Both dogs were splatched with white, the brindle was dead,
No white on this, and light enough yet remained
To show the autumn color and the hair's texture;
Here were the paws that killed the brindle and the calf;
In vain hunted; chance-met.

                    But Fera supposed
His weapon was in his room in the house, he'd slip

Into the house to fetch it and she'd have fled
When he returned; hunting alone up the twilight hill
Might he not even now discover a woman
In the beast's hide, pity that woman? Already in her mind
She wavered away from the necessity of death;
If Michal had not been present she might have stood up
And shown . . .
The stroke that ended her thought was aimed too low.
In the hunter's mind a more deep-chested victim
Stood in the dusk to be slain; what should have transpierced
The heart broke the left arm-bone against the shoulder
And spared the life.

                        He knew, as she fell. He seemed to himself
To have known even while he fired. That worm of terror
Strangled his mind so that he kept no memory
Of Cawdor and the others taking her into the house.
He was left in the dark with a bruised face, someone had struck him,
Oh very justly.

                        He rose and stood reeling
Like a boy whom bad companions have filled with sweetened
Liquor, to make him their evening sport. The yellow
Windows of the house wavered, he fought the sickness
And went in-doors. Someone stared at him passing
Up-stairs; he heard from the door her moaning breath.
Cawdor examined the wound, George held the lamp
Over the naked arm and breast, Concha
Was dipping a sponge: it was the dark clot
Stringing from the red sponge that overcame him.
Cawdor's face, like a rock to break on, turned
To say hoarsely "You bastard get out of this place,"
And turned back to the wound; terrible face in the lamp-shadow
Black as the blood-clot.

                        He stood outside the door
Half fainting against the wall. Wanted him to go?

Good God, did he want to stay? Michal came whispering:
"You can't do anything here; and I am afraid of father.
Please go. Please go. To-morrow I'll meet you somewhere.
Oh what can you do here?"

                                While he limped on the stairway
Fera's moan sharpened and became a voice.
He found himself out of doors; the blanket-roll
He had rolled ready to start to-morrow at dawn
Was in his hand. He looked for his rifle
On the ground between the shot and the mark, and stumbled over it
After he had failed to find it.

                              The sky had cleared
With its local suddenness, full of nail-sharp stars
And a frosty dust of shining; he went up the dim star-path
By the lone redwood into wide night. His usurped mind
Unheeding itself ran in its track of habit,
So that he went from the oaks as before, upward
The gravelly slope of spoiled granite to the Rock.
He soon gathered dead twigs and kindled a fire
On the dome of the Rock, wishing Michal might see it
And bring him word in the morning. The night had turned
Frostily cold with its cleared sky.

X

                              Fera's moan became vocal, she flapped
    the hurt arm, the hand
Lying still and hooked, the marbled flesh working between the shoulder and
    the elbow. Michal remembered
Her eagle in the fresh of its wound waving the broken flag: another one of
    Hood's rifle-shots. Cawdor
Gripped the shoulder quiet with his hand, and clinked in the basin
From his right hand the small red splinter of bone he had fished from the
    wound. Fera's eye-lids, that hung
Half open on arcs of opaque white, widened suddenly, and fluttered shut,
    and stood wide open,

The liquid pools of night in the rayed gray rings dilating and contracting
    like little hearts,
Each sparked with a minute image of the lamp above them. She tongued
    her lips and the dry teeth
And moved her head. "This must be life, this hot pain.
Oh, the bad hunter! I fail in everything, like my father." Cawdor looked
    sideways to place in his mind
The strips of a torn sheet laid ready, and smooth straight sticks of
    pinewood kindling fetched from the kitchen;
He pressed a ragful of pungent liquid to the wound's mouths. Fera lay quiet,
    but Michal trembled
To see her lips retract from the teeth, and hear the teeth creaking together.
    Then Fera whispered:
"Horse-liniment. Of course you would. It burns." But Cawdor answered:
    "Hold the lamp, Michal. George, hold her quiet."
He gripped with his hands the shoulder and the upper arm. Then Fera:
    "Oh God! Oh no! No . . . no . . .
I'll tell you anything . . ." The ends of the fracture were heard touching;
    but she writhing her body whipped over
In George's and Concha's hands; Cawdor held without failure but her
    movement baffled him, the ends of bone
Were heard slipping. He shifted his grasp and said to the others
    "Loose-handed fools. Hold firm." But Fera
Straining her chalky and diminished face, the earth-stain still unwashed on
    her cheek, clear of the pillow:
"Oh please. Dearest! I'll not hide anything. I'm not to blame." His mind was
    fixed on his work, yet even
While his muscles were setting themselves again her words entered his
    understanding. His grip relaxed;
He looked at her face, the eyes stared bright terror but the mouth
Attempting a fawning smile: "I'll tell you everything, dearest, but don't
    torture me. I thought I had tasted
Torture before. How little I knew." Her teeth chattered together and she
    said "He forced me. Hood forced me.
He threw me down under the laurel tree
And stopped my mouth with his hand. So that I couldn't be your wife any
    more, darling. But I
Never loved him. I only tried to be killed. Oh, Oh, his face

Is like a nigger's. George save me! Michal!" He sighed, "You lie. Be quiet."
   "Darling," she pleaded, "I feel

Pain so much more than you understand. I can't *bear* pain? *Bear* pain? I am
   not made like the people

You're used to." He wavered his head as if a fringe hung over the eyes, and
   bent to the wound, but she:

"I only tried to be killed." He muttered, "I don't kill women." And Fera:
   "You'd be so kind. Oh

But the darkness was sweet." And feeling his hands, "Oh Concha, she cried,
   I've told him everything and yet he'll hurt me.

Dear Concha pray to him for me, he used to love you. And I have never been
   mean to you because of that,

Concha." Then Cawdor suddenly turned to the Indian woman: "Is it true,
   what she says?" But Michal: "No, no,

Her mind," she stammered, "gone wrong. Ah you coward, Fera." "And what
   part," Cawdor said, "had *you* in the play?

By God, you all . . . When?" he said hoarsely to Fera. "Before he died," she
   answered, her breath hissing

In little pulses. He gathered his strength and said, "Out, Michal." And when
   she had gone: "Was it in this room,

Or his?" She answered "Under the laurel tree

He threw me down: I was not to blame not to blame more

Than a murdered man is." George said, "She is lying. Her madness is fear
   of pain. She is sick." "Though I've been played

For the fool of the world I know more than that. They make lies for
   pleasure but not

Get killed for pleasure. You sick whore does it hurt? Here is a different bed
   from the brown leaves

And the panting dog." Her face looking no bigger than a broken doll's on
   the pillow answered: "I knew

You'd kill me, I didn't think torture, why must I suffer alone? If I am to
   blame a little is he

Not rich with blame? He has got away I suppose. I swear by God I never
   consented to him.

It was all violence, violence . . . Have pity: no pity? Sweetheart: I never called
   you before: Sweetheart,

Have mercy on me." He stood as if to go out of the room; he was heard
   breathing, and slowly his hands

Crept to his throat. He turned and came back and said: "It is not to punish
   you.
I must set the bone. You can't stay here and be kept, you'll need both arms
   to live with. I will use all
Gentleness: but you lie still, it will be done in a moment. I'll send for the
   doctor, but when he comes
It will be too swollen perhaps for mending. Indeed I have other business.
   People take pain like bread
When their life needs it. After it is set the ache
Will quiet, you'll sleep."

                         Michal outside the door
Heard her screaming and went in; but then she had fainted
And Cawdor worked more easily. He bound the arm
And set the splints, and bound it again and passed
A leather belt about her body to fasten it
Against her side. He looked then at her face,
The dark lashes lying still, the parted white lips
Pencilled at the borders with fine blue lines,
Meek as a child's after the turn of fever
Folds its weakness in sleep. Concha prepared
To bathe the face but Cawdor: "Let her alone.
Let her have the poor mercy while it lasts.
Come George, I'll help you saddle. He'll come sooner
For you than another." He spoke quietly, but leaving
The room he walked against the wall by the door
And spread his hands both ways to feel the door-frame
Before he went out. He ran and found Hood's room
Empty, before he went with George to the stable.
"I think it has cleared," he said in the dark, "aren't the stars out?"
He saw the red star of Hood's fire on the Rock.
"Take your pick of the horses: I must go back
And warn the women: she will wake in delirium
And strain the bandages loose: I didn't speak of that,
That I remember? That I remember? Good-night,"
He said eagerly. He turned, then George went down
Alone, but Cawdor up the hill to the Rock
As one tortured with thirst toils up the sandhills

To the known rock spring. When he issued from the oaks
On the ridge of the steep neck of air-crumbled granite
The canyon redwoods were a stain of black shade
In the pit below, the gleam-powdered sky soared out of conception,
The starlight vastness and steepness were narrow to him
And no wind breathed. He was like one threading a tunnel
With anguished hunger of the air and light, all the arrows
Of desire strung to their heads on the pale spark
Of day at the end: so all the needs of his life
Hung on the speck of humanity by the red embers
On the rock dome. It heard him, and twitched and stood up.
He made in his mouth and waterless throat the words
"Come down," but no sound issued; he came nearer and said
"What did you steal? Come down." Hood screamed "Keep off,"
The same panic of brainless fear returning,
With a horror of his own cowardice, how could he bear
To run, but how could he bear to stand? He imagined
Fera had died. His very innocence of evil
Made the avenger unbearable, one of those hands
Could break his body, he snatched his rifle and stood
On the other side of the embers and sobbed "Stop there.
By God if you come nearer I'll fire. Keep off your hands.
I'm not hiding, I'll answer the law, not you.
I can't . . . Keep off. Oh! Oh!" For Cawdor blindly
Came through the fire; Hood with the rifle at his waist
Unshouldered, flung up the muzzle and shot in the air
Over his father's head: at the flash Cawdor
Felt a bright fear, not of death but of dying mocked,
Overreached and outraged as a fool dies,
Explode on his mind like light breaking on blindness
So that the body leaped and struck while the mind
Astonished with hatred stood still. There had been no choice,
Nor from the first any form of intention.
He saw Hood's body roll away from the fire
Like a thing with no hands; he felt in the knuckles
Of both his hands that both had been bruised on bone,
He saw Hood's body twist on the fall of the dome
Over the precipice and hands like weak flames

Scratch at the starlight rock: then one sharp moment's
Knife-edge a shadow of choice appeared: for all
Passed in a moment: he might have dived prone
And clutched after the hands with his hands: more likely
Gone down the granite slide into the gulf
With the other: but the choice had no consciousness
And in a moment no choice. There was no cry.
The curving hands scrabbled on the round of the rock
And slipped silently down, into so dreadful a depth
That no sound of the fall: nothing returned:
Mere silence, mere vanishing. Cawdor could hear the water
Whispering below, and saw the redwood forest
A long irregular stain in the starlit gorge-bottom,
But over the round of the rock it was not possible
To see the foot of the Rock. A little steady breeze
Blew curving up over the granite verge
From the night's drift in the chasm.

                              He turned and walked
Stealthily away, yet firmly, feeling no horror
But only a hollow unbearable sadness. But Hood had earned
The death he had got: not that he'd used violence
In adultery, that was incredible, the woman had lied:
But the crime however invited had no forgiveness,
Not even in death. Women are not responsible;
They are like children, little children grown lewd;
Men must acknowledge justice or their world falls
Piecemeal to dirty decay. Justice had been
Performed. He felt the sapping unbearable sadness
A little lightened, so muttered "Justice. Justice.
Justice": but the third time of saying it the word
Was pithed of meaning and became useless. He had come
Half way to the house and there remembered the things
Left on the Rock. He returned. Only his knowledge
Of what lay at the foot prevented him then
From casting himself down. Nor could he cast the rifle,
The silly rifle that Hood had loved,
For fear of its falling on the poor damned face.

He stood between the blanket-roll and the rifle
Beside a few burnt sticks and scattered red coals
On the bulge of the Rock. "Well, I have killed my son." Whether he
    continued living or quit living,
It would be a pity Michal should know. Quit, because it hurts? He thought
    he was not the make to do that.
His recent real temptation appeared a contemptible flourish of play-acting.
    "Well, I have killed my son.
He needed killing." The woman's story of the rape was now believed; it had
    become needful
To believe her story. "I will take these and bury them with him." When he'd
    again gone under the oaks
He heard one coming up the dark path. A moment of stupid horror he
    dreamed it was Hood coming
To claim the rifle. But Michal no doubt, Michal. He laid the things he
    carried into the darkness
Of the oaks by the path, and hardened his mind to meet Michal. Meet . . .
    whom? It brushed against the stiff leaves
Like something broken that crept and rested. With no terror but pity going
    down in the dark to meet it
He heard it snort and stamp hooves, a stray horse plunged from the path.
    "God damn you," he said and a voice answered
From down the path: "Hood, is that you?" She had been coming up to the
    Rock, and the strayed horse
Drifting ahead. She said "One of the horses: I guess it's gone. Oh Hood,
    Fera has said
Frightful . . . where are you?" She cried sharply "Who is that?" "The things
    were true," he answered, "all true." He heard her
Stop, and he seemed to feel her trembling. "Where's Hood," she said in a
    moment, trembling, "what have you done?"
"Nothing." He said in his heart "Well: I have killed him?" He possessed his
    voice in quietness and said, "I came
To ask him the truth, and he has confessed. It was all true." She sobbed and
    said "What have you done with him?"
"Nothing," he answered indifferently. "He ran when I came. A guilty
    conscience, Michal. He has done a thing
Never forgiven." He had reached her now; in the starless night of the oaks
    he saw the gleam of her face

Retreating, she moving slowly backward before him. He said "Like the scut
  of a deer." "What?" "When I came
He streaked up the hill into the starlight." "How did you make him
  confess?" "Oh Michal, a guilty conscience.
That does it. You know he wasn't a coward by nature, not a damned coward.
  I saw him run like a rabbit-scut
Between the hill and the stars. Come up to the Rock and call him." "I
  thought I heard a gun-shot," she faltered.
"I was in the house with . . . Then I went out." "A gun-shot? No. Come up
  and call him; perhaps he'll come down.
I promise you not to touch him. Come up and call to him, Michal. If you
  call loudly." They climbed to the Rock.
She saw it was vacant, the ends of a few sticks glowed on the stone, pale in
  their ash-crusts. "Hood. Hood,"
She called, and he said "Call louder. He has gone far." She answered,
"No, I won't call. I wish never to see him."

Who lay under the sheer below them, his broken shoulders
Bulging his coat in lumps the starlight regarded.
The bone vessel where all the nerves had met
For counsel while they were living, and the acts and thoughts
Been formed, was burst open, its gray and white jellies
Flung on the stones like liquor from a broken flask,
Mixed with some streamers of blood.

                                        The vivid consciousness
That waking or dreaming, its twenty years, infallibly
Felt itself unitary, was now divided:
Like the dispersion of a broken hive: the brain-cells
And rent fragments of cells finding
After their communal festival of life particular deaths.
In their deaths they dreamed a moment, the unspent chemistry
Of life resolving its powers; some in the cold star-gleam,
Some in the cooling darkness in the crushed skull.
But shine and shade were indifferent to them, their dreams
Determined by temperatures, access of air,
Wetness or drying, as the work of the autolytic
Enzymes of the last hunger hasted or failed.

Yet there appeared, whether by chance or whether
From causes in their common origin and recent union,
A rhythmic sympathy among the particular dreams.
A wave of many minute delicious enjoyments
Would travel across the spilth; then a sad fading
Would follow it, a wave of infinitesimal pains,
And a pause, and the pleasures again. These waves both lessened
In power and slowed in time; the fragments of consciousness
Beginning to lapse out of the frailties of life
And enter another condition. The strained peace
Of the rock has no repose, it is wild and shuddering, it travels
In the teeth of locked strains unimaginable paths;
It is full of desire; but the brittle iniquities of pleasure
And pain are not there. These fragments now approached
What they would enter in a moment, the peace of the earth.

XI

When Cawdor had left the house, Concha
At once busied herself to recall to life
The milk-faced bandaged one on the bed, then Michal
Had intervened: "He said to let her alone.
He said to let her have peace." But Concha: "She stay
Fainting too long, she stop breathing, she die."
"I think that would be better." But the Indian woman
Trembling went on, then Michal held up the basin
While the other bathed the pale face, gray jewels of water
Ran down in the hair. There was no response; then Michal
Herself began to be frightened. She knew that her father
Had kept a bottle of whiskey somewhere in the room;
She set the basin on the blue chair and went
Searching on shelves.

            Concha flung back the sheet
And blanket to bathe the breast. How the hard strap
That held the arm furrowed the flesh of the waist.
The fine-grained clear white skin was beautiful to her;
The coins of rose about the small nipples

Astonished her; hers were as black as the earth; she dipped her head
As if to a flower's fragrance and felt the quiet breasts
She had cooled with water move on her face: Fera
Moaned and then said faintly, "You are blind, father.
Both horses were white." She moved her head on her hair,
Her voice changed: "Do you love me Concha? You never were jealous,
I've wondered at you. Where's Cawdor?" Michal returned
And said sullenly: "I've found it, and there's no glass.
She'd better suck from the bottle." But Fera lay
Regardless of her, and dropping her right forearm
Across her breast explored the splints, and folds
On heavy folds of linen that shelled the shoulder
And the left arm; then with pain-dwindled lips,
"Well," she said, "give it to me. It's time for me now
To taste of my father's friend. Help me sit up, Concha."
She sipped and choked; it spilled on her chin, the burning fragrance
Filled all the room. Michal took back the bottle
And said, "Why did you lie? You lied. You lied.
Horrible things." Fera dull-eyed, with racked mouth,
The coughing had hurt her arm: "Not lies. Every word
Faithful as death. I lay between your father and your brother
Like a snake between the rock and the stone.
Give me the bottle, give it back to me Michal.
I have to hush this torment. Your father'll come back
And beat me with his fists like a wild beast,
He's like a beast in his rages." "Every word's lies.
But if it were true, why did you tell him?" "Because he tortured me."
Michal crossed the room to the corner and saw
In the east window high up in the dark pane
A little drop of red light. She pressed her face
Against the glass and cupped it with her two hands
To shut the lamplight away. Hood's waning fire,
Like a red star under the diamond stars.
"I'll go and ask him," she said turning. "He'll tell me
Every last word was a lie." "What did you see, Oh what did you see,
    Michal?"
Fera said shaking. "A fire on the Rock? It's only some vaquero from inland,
    Hood wouldn't build one,

Not to-night, not to-night." She answered "I saw nothing. I saw the sky
　　and some stars. Concha,
Take care of her, will you. Get her to sleep." As Michal crossed to the door
　　a dim noise like a gun-shot
Seemed to be heard, she said "Oh, what was that? Concha: you heard it?
　　Listen." But Fera laughing
With an ashen face: "Lived here all her life long
And never has heard a wave slapping the sand at the creek-mouth."

　　　　　　　　　　　　　　　　　　　　　　　　When she'd
　　gone out, Fera said: "Concha,
My father's blindness was crystal to hers. How could she stay in the room
　　and let Cawdor go out
To find his prey in the night? Did she know *nothing*? Give me the bottle,
　　dear Concha. Dear Concha." She drank,
And said: "I'd no other way to keep him, he was going away. Poor hunter.
　　I set a beast on his track
That he's no match for. The gun's no good boy hunter, you might as well
　　toss acorns. Two bulls, Concha,
Fighting by starlight, the young one is gored. Ah: Concha:
One of my loves was locked in the hill by the oak, now the other's safe too.
　　Listen: my birthday's to-night.
Has to be kept," she stammered, "I've told no one but you. And here's my
　　father's friend to sit up with.
Go down and get two glasses, Concha, and a pitcher of water." She called
　　her back from the door. "Concha!
The water in the house is all stale.
Go out to the spring among the calla lilies
And fill the pitcher. Don't hurry, Concha, I'm resting now."

　　　　　　　　　　　　　　　　　　　　　　　　As Concha
　　went out Fera stealthily
Undid the belt that locked her arm to her side; when the Indian was gone
She passed one-handed the strap through the buckle, the tongue thrown
　　back
To let it slide free. She knotted the end of the strap
To the top of the carved bed-post, kneeling on the pillow,
Tightening the knot between her hand and her teeth.

She dropped the collar about her neck, and shuffled her knees
Until they slipped from the mattress. The right arm
Sustained the left one, to ease its pain in the fall.
She could have breathed by standing, but while her mind
Remained she would not, and then was unable.

                                    Concha, down-stairs,
Had much to tell Ilaria. Acanna was there too
In the kitchen, and Concha's boy Romano, and Dante
Vitello, the Swiss. All questioned her. She'd forgotten
The water and found the glasses, when little Romano
In his child voice: "Escucha: un raton. — Listen mother,
A mouse in the ceiling." But no one looked up nor down
Until he fetched the gray cat from under the stove
And wanted to take her up-stairs. Concha forbade him,
But listened, and heard the noise in the ceiling change
From a soft stroking to a dull shudder in the wood.
The shudder was Fera's agony; the backs of her feet
Stroking the floor; she hung as if kneeling. But Concha said:
"A trade-rat maybe: no mouse. But I must go up."
The noise had ceased.

                            She screamed in the hallway above
And flung the glasses on the floor. The people below
Stared at each other. Her cries were timed, rhythmic,
Mechanical, like a ground-squirrel's when he sits up
Beside his burrow and watches a dog hunting
On the other side of the fence. At length Acanna
Ran to the stair, the others followed, and little Romano
With gray puss in his arms. They looked past Concha
Who stood in the door not daring to enter.

                                        The girl
Appeared kneeling, only her knees were lifted
A little above the floor; her head devoutly
Drooped over. She was naked but the bandaged arm;
The coins about the small nipples were now
As black as Concha's; the lips dark, the fine skin

Mottled with lead-color. Ilaria pushed in and lifted
The body, Jesus Acanna then found his knife
And cut the strap. They stretched the slender body
On the bed and began to talk, but Dante Vitello
Remembered at length to pump the ribs with his hands.
They saw the lids of the eyes after a time
Flutter and close; the Swiss paused from his labor,
The breathing went on by itself.

                    Cawdor returned
From the Rock with Michal, but would not enter the house.
He seemed going toward the sea when she left him. He went
As far as the work-shop and fetched tools for digging,
A lantern, matches to light it. He chose the tools
With a clear mind; this work had to be done
Because of the coyotes. It proved more dreadful
Than he'd imagined; but when it was done the dreadfulness itself
Had purged his mind of emotion. He took no pains
To conceal the grave, for at this time discovery
Meant nothing to him, he desired nor feared nothing,
Not even to put back time and undo an act.
However, no person ever went up there.
He rolled stones on the grave against the coyotes,
And gathered the tools, but when he had carried them
Half way home, he threw them with the lantern too
Into the creek under the starless redwoods.
His mind ceased there, as if the tools had been strings
Between the world and his mind; these cut, it closed.

In the bright of dawn, before sunrise began,
The lank steers wheeled their line when he waved his arms.
He cursed them with obscene words . . . but why? . . . and there stood
Thirty in a row, all in a row like soldiers
Staring at him with strained-up heads. He was in the pasture
On the highest dome of the hill.
Wild fragrant wind blew from the burning east,
A handful of cloud high up in the air caught fire and vanished.
A point of more excessive light appeared

On the ridge by the lone oak and enlarged.
Without doubt, the sun. But if it were the horn of a flaming beast:
We'd have a horned beast to see by.
"What have I lost by doing through a blind accident
What I ought to have done in cold blood? Was Hood anything to me?
I have lost nothing." He'd have counted Fera
Lost, if he'd thought of Fera; she did not enter his mind.
"If I'd lost much: it's likely I'd not lie down
But gather again and go on." His flesh and bones were soaked
With aching weariness: but that was nothing either.
His eyes dazzled in the rivers of light
And the sea lay at his feet flat and lifeless
Far down but flecked with the steps of the wind. He went down to the
    house
And heard that Fera had hanged herself and been saved,
But that was nothing either. No, something. Where were you?
He said to Concha. "She send me down. She send me.
She send me down for water. When I come back: Oh!"
"I'll not see her this morning," he answered.
"Bring my clothes to the little room on the north
And change the bed there. Hood's gone for good." He had done justly,
And could sleep very well there.

                              Two days passed
Before he remembered the blanket-roll and the rifle
Dropped in the oaks when Michal came. He went and sought
But never found them. But that was nothing either.

XII

Her voice was still roughened with an off whisper
In the bruised throat, and the white of one of her eyes
Grained with a drop of red, a little blood-vessel
Had broken there when the strap drew. When she was alone
She lay pointed on the bed, stiffened to the attitude
Of formal death, feeling the ache in her arm
But hardly conscious of it, the hours and scenes
And the form as a whole of all her life incessantly

Moving behind the blank wide open eyes.
She lay and contemplated it with little emotion
And hardly a thought. She thought of herself as dead,
Although she knew perfectly that she was living,
And had said to Concha: "You needn't watch me, you and Ilaria.
I'll never try death again, now I understand
That to fail is the very soul of my soul.
Failure is not so sweet that one who feels it
Beforehand will go running to meet it again.
Though death is sweet. That will come in its time
When I'm as old as my father, I fear not sooner;
Never for the asking."

                       She said to Concha another day:
"I wish you could get Michal to come and see me;
Or George even. Not one soul has come in,
Not since the doctor was here, and death is so lonesome.
I could get up, but when I begin to walk
Cawdor will send me away. You must never tell them
That I can get up." This was at noon; Concha
Painfully made a slow thought in her mind
All afternoon, and said to Cawdor in the evening,
Stammering, because her words were planned beforehand:
"She say that she is well enough to get up."
"Who says?" "Oh . . . she . . ." "You mean," he said frowning,
"My wife? Let her get up then." She turned sadly, and then said:
"When she get up you going to send her away?"
"What is that to you?" Then Concha recklessly: "You keep her
After she loving with Hood?" She curved her body
In fear of his hand; but he took hold of her wrist
And drove her up the stairway to Fera's room.

Who lay in the bed straightened to the shape of death
And looked at them with still eyes; the scarlet drop
In the white of the left one spoiled her eyes' peace. Cawdor
Put off the questions that had burned him to ask,
And stood still and then said: "You are well enough to get up,
Concha says, but you think I'd send you away."

She smiled at Concha. "I wondered whether you'd do it.
And then I thought you wouldn't, but it's no matter.
No: you won't send me," she said to Cawdor, "for I
Suffered my destruction in simple innocence.
Oh, certainly you'll not drink again from a mouthed cup,
But the cup's not blamed. You are much too just to punish the cup. There
    are more reasons." His face a moment
Was like her father's a scar; it formed itself to be dark metal again and he
    said: "No doubt
You were loving with him and so he went mad." She thought, and answered:
    "No. You did justice. I know what you did.
You'd better send out your brown tattle-tales
Before we say any more, she'd hear and go tell, wouldn't you Concha?
    Besides that her sour odor
Poisons the room. I've noticed lately, the living smell much worse than the
    dead. Oh never mourn them;
No one was ever sorry to have died." He shook his head, like the bull that
    has charged a man and found
Only the vacant flapping of a red blanket, and he said: "Be straight will you
    for once, I won't hurt you.
You hide in a smoke of words like lies. Perhaps" — his face hollowed with
    terror — "it was all a lie?
No, that can't be. You white poison you were in the boat with him and lied
To save your skin?" He turned on Concha: "Did you see her make love to
    him?" But the Indian woman feared to go on;
She shook her head, and looked aside at Fera, and shook her head. Cawdor
    made himself patient
And said, "Perhaps a kiss: or you saw her stroking his head: he had fine
    hair . . ." Fera lay faintly
Smiling and watched him; he looked, stooping his face to Concha's, like a
    tall old Jew bargaining, and said:
"Or you saw them . . . by God, you told me they kissed, you said that."
    She nodded her head, panting and shrinking backward,
Wiping her dark hands on her apron incessantly; and Fera: "She'll tell more
    lies if you make more faces,
And when that fails you could pinch her arm. How can you expect truth
    from such people, they're all afraid of you?"

He looked at Concha and said feebly: "If I could know.
I am stupid and things are hidden. What I have done. Was right, but the
    blood rushes me behind my eyes
And God sends chance. It all happened in the blindness of chance." Fera
    said quietly "Don't talk before her."
He looked at her eyes and said, "You have the secret, if I could trust you.
    That red drop comes from hanging
And will clear up. You seem quieter in mind
Than ever before. Do you know where I sleep now? Hood's room." "It was
    Concha's first." He groaned in his throat, feeling
That every thought in her mind was impure, how could he fish the truth
    from a dirty fountain? He said:
"And yet you'll tell me. It will make no difference to you but only to me. I
    will do nothing to punish you,
Whatever you say, nothing in your favor either." "I've told you already," she
    answered. "But whether you tempted him,
Invited him, you egged him on, you thought he was safe. A word: or only a
    damned smile: women
Can move hell with their eyes." She closed her eyes, and said keeping them
    closed: "What I said that night
Each word was true. You're right though, I've still a secret. Shoo tattle-tales
    out,
And then I'll tell you my secret." He said, "Concha: get out." She sighed
    and went out gladly, and Fera:
"Open the door; I won't have her at the door." However the hallway was
    empty, and Fera said:
"I was friendly with him, he was your son and Michal's brother. I never in
    act nor look nor thought
Stepped over that. Was he vicious when he was little? I never knew it.
    A beast lived in his blood,
But no one warned me and now he is gone." "That's the word: gone. You
    are safe to blacken him, he can't answer."
"If I should lie and whiten him," she said,
"And say he was innocent, some stitch of his nerves in him destroyed me
    but his heart was innocent: and you believed it:
How could you sleep? And after a night or two
That room you have taken might seem too little for you. You are very
    strong, you'd hold yourself quiet three nights,

Or four nights, and then wander on the hill scaring the cattle." He said
   gravely, "Does every one know?
Who told you this?" "No one," she answered. "And after a week of nights
   they'd find you with those big-boned
Fingers clenched in your throat quiet on the hill." "On the Rock," he said.
   "Oh, on the Rock. But since . . .
Or under the Rock. But since he was guilty you can sleep sound." The flesh
   of his face, that had sagged lately,
Was now become firm for danger, and he asked: "How do you know these
   things if no one watched me?" She answered
"I know you so well. I used to be near you, if you remember, before I was
   spoiled. And now, lying
Like this" — she lay pointed in the bed, her arms on her breast — "I mean
   alone and cut off from life,
I've had leisure and power to think of you plainly, so all your acts that night
   stand in my mind
Fixed and forever like pieces of stone. That's the way with us dead, we see
   things whole and never
Wonder at things." He said, "You lie here and dream and imagine. There's
   nothing in it." "So you won't send me,"
She answered, "to stay with strangers. I know too much and might tell:
   that's nothing to you: but as time darkens
You'll find me the only comforter you have. And I can teach you the way to
   blessedness: I've tasted life
And tasted death; the one's warm water, yellow with mud and wrigglers,
   sucked from a puddle in the road,
Or hot water that scalds you to screaming;
The other is bright and cool and quiet, drawn from the deep. You knocked
   the scummed cup from the boy's hand
And gave him the other: is that a thing to be sorry for? I know; I have both
   in my hands; life's on the broken
And splinted left so I never lift it. You did kindly, not terribly. If you were
   wise, you'd do
As much for yourself. If you were loving you'd do
As much for me." He stood and listened, and said "Is that all?"
She nodded. "Then it's not much.
I see there are two of us here twisting in hell,
Smile as you like." "Why yes," she answered, "by the left arm.

That's true. But I taste both." He was leaving the room
And she cried after him: "Oh my dear, dear, be merciful.
Life is so tough to cut, I never would have dreamed.
I fail. But nothing stops *you*."

                      He went out-doors
And felt a seeming-irresistible desire
To go to the foot of the Rock and lie with those stones
On the soft earth, his mouth whispering against it.
But now, he must never give in to any desire;
Strain the iron forever. Never do anything strange:
For even now their eyes followed him strangely.
No matter; they'd keep in subjection; they might have watched it
And not dare speak: but a pity if little Michal . . .
The stars in the sparse boughs, the skies are never
Darkened any more, a naughty glitter.
How does one commonly spend a winter evening:
Not letting the stars glitter through the split boughs.
He entered the house and sat down. Strain the iron forever:
He had strength for that.

                    Fera had little strength,
And the long hollow night coming looked unendurable.
Her right arm was flung free of the cover and lay
Bent on her eyes; after a while her teeth
Found the wrist: ugh, what was this? She raised it and saw
The yellow and brown scabs of the laceration
Where she had gnawed it before.

                     In the morning, when Concha
Came in to serve her, she said "Did you believe in heaven and hell
When you were little? (To-day I'll get up,
I've had enough of this bed, you'll help me dress.)
Because you know the dead rarely come back;
But I died and came back, and I can tell you
More than the priests know. Dying's not bad: Oh, bad enough,
But you can stand it, you have to. But afterwards . . . Ah, there's . . ."
She moaned, her tight small fist crept up to her cheek

And trembled there. She was playing a comedy, she played it so well
Her own flesh suffered and chilled. "Death is no sleep, Concha, death is
   eternal torment and terror
For all that die. Neither is there any heaven for anyone. I saw my father
   there crying blood
From the hollows of his blind eyes and tearing his beard with his hands. He
   said 'Oh my God have you come, Fera?
Who ever dreamed that death could be worse than life?' I said 'It is so,' and
   all the crowd of the dead
Began moaning 'It is so.' But then you managed to make me breathe with
   your hands and I could come back,
They said to me then, 'Never tell any living person what death is like, for if
   they imagined
What it's like, for they all must come, how could they live?
Who'd not go mad with fear to feel it approaching?'
Oh Concha, hug life with tooth and nail, for what
Comes after is the most horrible. And no end, no end.
(Come here and help me. We'll have to slit down the sleeve
And pin it over the shoulder.) I didn't tell you
To scare you, Concha. Don't think about it. Ah no,
Or we'd sit screaming.
I wasn't going to tell you but then I thought
That you can bear it as well as I can, after the trick
You played me last night, my rival!
Live. Live forever if you could. Oh it was frightful."

XIII

Though she was up, and began to live and go out,
She avoided Cawdor's presence, still fearing to be sent away
If seen too often. She kept her room at mealtimes,
And he was almost never about the house
The other hours of the day.

                    The first time she went out,
She only walked under the storm-broken cypresses
About the door and went in; but the next morning
She climbed the steep to the great oak by the graves.

Still weak and bloodless, dizzy with climbing, she lay
Face down on the dug earth, her mouth breathing against it
And whispering over her father's body below.
The grave retained its freshness, no rain had fallen
On the red earth. She heard after a time
A rustling and scraping noise and raised her head.
It was Michal's eagle hungrily astir in the cage;
She used to feed it about this time. Fera
Saw beak and eyes in the shadow, and the dark square
Of the box cage against the bright blue shining
Flat ocean and the arch of sky. She stood up, and walked
About the oak's bole; she seemed to be counting the graves,
But there were only three; the two ancient ones
Enclosed with pickets and the raw new one unfenced.

Michal came up with flesh and water for the eagle,
But Fera stood on the other side of the oak
Until she had come; then, coming forward from it:
"Why Michal, how strange to think that all these days,
No matter what's happened, you still go on steadily as sunrise.
My father dies of old age, I fish for death
And catch failure again, and Hood . . . but you and the sunrises
Go on as if our tears and our deaths were nothing.
He isn't glad to see you: I'd have been glad to see you
My lonely days in bed but you never came."
Michal had looked over her shoulder, her face
Growing white as it turned. She turned back to the cage.
"I didn't know you were here," she said, and poured out
The dirty water from the drinking-basin
Without turning again. "I see that you hate me,"
Fera said; "we'll not speak of that. I see that your father
Has thought *my* father's grave not worthy of a mark.
If the cold charity of the county had buried him
There'd be a stake with his name.
Yet he was here like a man among cattle,
The only mind in this ditch." Michal said nothing,
But rubbed the white slime from the basin and rinsed it,
And Fera said, "The oak's dying, they chopped its roots.

Or was it the storm that burned these baby leaves?
We ought to be friends, Michal." Michal set in
The filled basin and shut the door of the cage.
She opened her lips to speak, and then kept silence,
And Fera said "You'll listen, my dear, if you won't speak. Do you think I'll swallow
These white and hating looks as if they were earned? What have I done? Tried to die? Yes; I tried twice;
And that was stupid, but people are pitied for that, not hated. You were quite kind my days of sunshine,
And now you peck the feathers from the sick bird." Michal said trembling, "Oh, no. Not that I'm spiteful,
Only, I can't understand." "That's true," she answered, "how could you?
Your life has been sweet and full of ignorance. But I, when my father was drunk in town, would hear my mother
Take lovers in the house. *There* was somebody to hate. Yet they were white men;
They weren't the color of Concha . . . no more of that. The second time I died I almost made it, you know.
They pumped me alive with their hands and I was born again
From the dark air: since then I can understand much that was dark before. So you, Michal,
Will understand . . . many things that are dark . . . when some wild night kills childhood in you. That's coming:
But don't pray for it, my dear.
Oh Michal that's the reason I so much want you to listen to me. The inflamed and dark season
And bitterness will come, and then I dread your saying to yourself: 'Fera she hated life; Fera
Preferred death; Fera was wise.' I wasn't; at least you mustn't think so. I welched on my fate,
(And failed of course, failure's my root in nature) but I am ashamed. So you must listen to me, Michal,
My praise of life, by my dead father, by the dying oak. What I've lived has not been lucky you know,
If I can praise it, who'd not? But how good it is, Michal, to live! Good for what? Ah, there's the question.

For the pleasure of it? Hardly for that. Take your own life, mine's marked,
    mine's worse than usual. Your mother
Lies yonder; you never knew her, you missed the *pleasure* of knowing her.
    You missed the pains too; you might have hated her.
More likely you'd have loved her deeply; you'd have been sad then to see her
    wasting with age and pain,
Those years would come; and you'd have felt the salt fountains of loneliness
Drain from your eyes when the day came and she died. There's not a
    pleasure in the world not paid for, Michal,
In pain with a penny or two for interest. But youth, they say, is a shining
    time, and no doubt for you
The pleasures outsun the pains. Then the hair grays, and the teeth blacken
    or drop, and the sky blackens.
You've swollen ankles and shrunk thighs, and horrible hanging breasts that
    flap like a hound's ears,
Or death comes first . . . Oh, but I'm wrong, it's life I was praising! And the
    pain to the pleasure is sun to candle.
Joy never kills, you know, the most violent joy
Never drove anyone mad. Pain kills, and pain drives mad; and extreme pain
    can feed for days
On the stretched flesh; the extremes of pleasure rot in two minutes.

                                                                  Oh yes,
        but, Michal,
Surely life's . . . good? My father — his thoughts were deep,
Patient and wise — believed it was good because it was growing.
At first it was a morsel of slime on the sea,
It grew to be worms and fishes, lizards and snakes,
You see the progress, then things with hair and hot blood,
It was coming up from the ocean and climbing mountains,
Subduing the earth, moulding its bundle of nerves
Into the magnificent mind of man, and passing
Beyond man, to more wonders. That helped my father!
He loved that. You and me of course it can't help,
Because we know nothing goes on forever.
What good is better and better if best draws blank?
Here's the oak was growing upward a hundred years

And now it withers. Sometime the world
Will change, only a little too hot or too cold
Or too dry, and then life will go like the oak.
Then what will all my father's magnificent thoughts,
Michal, and all the dreams of your children be worth?
Well, we must praise life for some other reason.
For surely it's . . . good? We know it must be. Here every morning
You bring food to this bird to keep it alive:
Because you love it: in its filth, in misery, in prison. What's wretcheder than
     a caged eagle? Guess. I'll not tell.
And you'd be bitter cruel to keep it alive: sick-feathered, abject,
     broken-armed: only, you know
Life is so *good*. It's true the creature seems ungrateful: but I am not grateful
     either: to Dante
Vitello who pumped the breath into my body."
She stopped and looked at Michal's white face, and said
"You haven't heard from Hood yet? He went so suddenly,
He ought to write you." Michal said "No," and Fera:
"You know nothing about him?" She cried trembling:
"Why do you ask about Hood? Why do you ask about Hood?
Let me alone." "Ah," Fera said, "do you think
That something has happened to him?" "He'll never come back.
It was your fault." "I'm sure he'll never come back,"
She said with a still face. "Now let's go down.
But I can't joke about your eagle Michal.
The hopeless cage of pain is a lamp
Shining rays that go right through the flesh
And etch the secrets of bone. Mine aches. Oh no, Michal,
I couldn't do it: but George would kill him for you:
Or ask your father: that's better: those are the hands."

Another morning Fera went up
Secretly under the redwoods to the Rock's foot,
Where the great ribbed and battering granite face
Came down and found earth. In spring the cliff-swallows nest
A third of the way up, and a pair of duckhawks
Two thirds of the way. High in air the gray dome
Seemed swaying from the sweep of the small fibrous clouds.

Fera crept back and forth at the foot with pale
Spying eyes: but this loose earth was only a squirrel's mound,
And that was a gopher's digging: for hours: and she found
Stones had been rolled together, their brown earth-bellies
Turned up to the sky, and the gray lichenous backs
Downward, there was fresh earth below, with grass-blades
Half buried and ferns trampled. One rain had fallen.
She stood and gazed and said to him there: "Did I not say beforehand
That after we were dead I should have no rest after all but run moaning
On the gray shore, gnawing for my hunger a wrist of shadow?" She found a
    brown scurf on the slope rocks
Above, and thought, "This is the blood that burst from your mouth when
    you fell"; caressing with hers the doubtful
Crust, that was really a brown lichen. "Oh why would you not listen to me?
    You chose, to die
Rather than live. Ah, you'd learned wisdom somewhere, you were too young
    to be wise, when with one beautiful
Act of delight, lovely to the giver as the taker, you might have made
A star for yourself and for me salvation." She rose and said to the grave:
    "It was I that killed you. The old man
Who lives in hell for it was only my hands."

XIV

It was true; and it was Cawdor that paid the suffering.
The woman found ease in words and outcry; the man,
The more sensitive by sex and by his nature,
Had forbidden himself action because one act
Was grown his cancer; speech because speech betrays;
Even thought, in one regard, for if Hood's guilt
Were not monstrous the punishment became monstrous,
And if he had been solicited into adultery
His guilt was not monstrous but halved and natural;
There was evidence enough for that, and there
Thought was forbidden. Meanwhile his mind remained
Implacably clear for the rest, cloudless harsh light
On what he had done, memory not dimmed with time
But magnified and more real, not masked with any

Mysticism, that comes most often and stands
Between the criminal and his crime, a redeemer
Shifting the load onto fate; no failure toward unreason
Except the fantasy of his wife's innocence.

His loved canyon was grown hateful and terrible;
He longed to go away, go away, but that
Was cowardice, the set pride and code of his life
Prohibited that; he desired to kill himself,
But that was cowardice; to go and accuse himself,
But that was a kind of cowardice; all the outlets of action
Were locked and locked. But the most present desire,
And the most self-despised, was to ask advice
No matter of whom: of George, of Dante Vitello:
He yearned on them with his eyes: but that was cowardice
And ridiculous too. Day by day the tensions of his mind
Were screwed tighter in silence. He had some strength,
Though not the strength his vanity used to imagine,
And now in the deadlock of his powers endurance
Continued still. He felt the eyes of his house
That used to peer at him from behind now openly
Glitter before his face. He believed they all knew,
Save little Michal, and were kept quiet by fear,
They watched his face for weakness, as the blackbirds
In Carmel Valley watch the green fruit for softness.

After the flood in December the later rains
Fell scant, shrewd north wind heeling listless falls
Blew the hills dry; Cawdor discovered his mind
Building conjectural bridges between the drought
And the curse of his deed; he conquered the sick thought,
Another cowardice.

                    In March when the cows were calving
Came printed news of foot-and-mouth disease
Among the cattle in the north, it had come in
Through San Francisco from Asia. An infected herd
Had been destroyed. Cawdor read and feared nothing,

His herd in the isolation of the coast canyon
Would be the last. Yet he dreamed in the night
That he was slaughtering his herd. A bench was dug
To stand on, in the steep wall of a gully;
He stood there with the sledge-hammer and Jesus Acanna
All black on a black horse against the twilight
Drove in the cattle. One swing of the hammer for each
On the peak between the horns, but the white-faced heifer
Sidled her head and the blow crushed the horn.
Bawling and slopped with blood down the sleek shoulders,
Plunging among the carcasses . . . The dream returned
Too many times; the plague increasing in the north
He warned his men to guard the pasture and watch
For strays; then the dream ceased; but the hurt heifer
Still troubled his dreams.

     His mind had relented toward Fera,
Innocent sufferer and as wretched as himself.
He saw now that both George and Michal hated her.
Her arm had knitted crooked, it pained always
In her pale eyes. He spoke to her kindly; she answered patiently.
He saw as in a vision that if he should choose
He might go back to his own room from Hood's
This very night, and all be as it was before.
To hell with the glittering eyes, they would keep quiet.
"No," he said and went out of the house. But she
Followed and overtook him under the cypresses
In the evening twilight.

    Michal and George were left
In the lamplight in the room, and Michal said
"I want you . . ." she made more words but they were too mumbled
To understand; she stopped and drew breath and said
Astonishingly aloud, as if she were calling
Across a canyon: "I want you to kill my eagle.
I ought never to have kept it. Nothing but wretchedness.
George, will you kill it quickly and without pain
To-morrow morning?" He stared at her and said

"We've other troubles to think of." "Yes. If you won't
I'll do it myself." "I will. Don't cry, Michal."
She went up-stairs crying.

                              In the twilight under the trees
Fera touched Cawdor's arm and said timidly: "The best
Would be not to've been born at all; but if we are bound to live why should
    we hate each other?"
He turned in surprise, he had forgotten her. "You are not bound." "By
    failures of nature. I am like a sick beast . . .
Like Michal's eagle . . . I can't do for myself. I've tried. Think of *me* a little.
    You did the other
No evil but eternal good. Forget him now, and if I can't end: failure's my
    peg that I hang on:
Mayn't we go back and live as we were before? You loved me once, when
    I was a child and you
Were a man." He stood silent thinking of another matter, suddenly he
    barked with laughter and said
"What am I now?" "A living God: you could answer prayer if you pleased."
    "Don't be troubled," he said,
"About God. You talk about God
The day before you go mad." "I can't do that either. Are you afraid to live,"
    she answered,
"Because they whisper? But they know nothing; they've not a thread of
    evidence. I've talked to them all, not one
But I, not one but I could betray you." She peered up at his face to see
    what it said in the twilight.
It said nothing; he was thinking of another matter, and walking the open
    way from the trees, slowly
Toward the sea's fading light. "Besides, they are all afraid of you. Oh listen!"
    she said. "We two alone
Have all the decision. Nobody but I can twitch the reins in your hands.
    Look at me." She caught his arm.
"Am I changed?" He looked, and suddenly laughed with pleasure. "Why . . .
    like a blown-out candle. Perfectly changed.
The fragrance all gone, all the wind fallen." He failed to see the lightning
    pallor, he was so prisoned

In the surprise of his mind. "No more in my eyes than a dead stick. No
   more," he said in astonishment,
"Than Concha Rosas." He spoke with no intention of cruelty, his mind in
   the pain of its own bonds
Islanded alone, incapable of feeling another's. She clasped her throat with
   her hand and said shuddering:
"For this. No, not another time.
I went on my knees to Hood, I made myself a shameless beggar, I washed
   his feet with tears.
That's not done twice. To love me: and he would not.
Ah God how can I make you know it? I duped you too well. Ah dupe, Ah
   fool," she stammered, "Ah murderer.
Machine that one winds up and it goes and does it. I wound you, I was the
   one. Now the air's fire
To drink and the days and nights the teeth and throat of a dog: shall I hide
   your eyes with my hand always
From what you have done, to let you die in sweet ignorance?" He said "Go
   on. Strain it out, gasping, a heifer
With the first calf." "It's the only child I'll bear you. I hope you will like the
   child. You killed the other
Woman's but mine perhaps will spill *you*
From the same rock. For proofs: ask Michal, she heard me pray to him for
   love: ask Concha Rosas again,
The fat beast listened and saw, she heard me, she helped me fool you: ask
   Jesus Acanna,
Watched me lead Hood from my father's earth to the laurel to be my lover:
   I led him, *I* called him, *I* flung
Flowers and fire at his feet: he never at mine: and he refused me, he died for
   that. Ask your eyes,
Heartless blue stones in their caves, wanted to be blind and they saw,
They saw me come down in the rain to call him, the rain steamed where it
   struck, I was hot, I walked in a shameless
Burning heat; my father was dying but I ran down.
And again you saw me, Hood was naked in bed at dawn, you caught me in
   his room. Had he received me
Gladly or kindly, had he raised his arms to receive me? I begged and he put
   me by, I broke in to beg

And he was driving me out when you came. He remembered his father's
   honor, he was a fool and faithful,
He's paid for it, he was faithful to you, you paid the wages. Ah, wait, I've
   more.
It's precious to me to tell you these things, I've hardly desired honey-sweet
   death a longer while."
"You lie too much," he answered, "I asked you before to tell me. Pour it
   out."
He stood like a gray tree in the twilight, only a surface trembling, the axe
   was blunted in the bark,
Fera thought; and she said: "I asked him to cut leaves from the laurel to lay
   in my father's grave,
There are no flowers in this ditch,
And under the laurel I gave him my love. Are you glad that he had my love?
   That saves you, that lets you live.
The old husband happy in his wife's pleasures.
Under the laurel it was, behind the concealing oaks, under the laurel it was.
   Before,
I had only cried out and begged with tears, but there I gave him my body,
   my arms about him, my breasts
Against him: be patient will you, this is not much, this is not the poison:
   I gave him my flesh to eat,
As Michal takes up meat to the eagle, but he was wilder than the eagle.
He remembered his father's honor, he would not feed. My arms were his
   cage, I held the meat to his mouth,
He would not feed." Her face distorted itself and seemed to reflect flame,
   like the white smoke
Of a hidden fire of green wood shining at night, twisting as it rises. Gipsies
   crouch by the smoke's root
Watching strange flesh simmer in the pot between the forked sticks. When
   the wind varies their eyes prickle
And the shine of the smoke hides the gray stars. Her face writhed like the
   shining smoke and she cried and said:
"I wish the little rivers under the laughing kingfishers in every canyon were
   fire, and the ocean
Fire, and my heart not afraid to go down.
I broke my heart against his mouth like honeycomb, he would not take me,
   Oh the bitter honey, the black-blooded

Drops from the wax, no wonder he refused me. There was a lion-skin
I wore to my death, was it you stole it or Concha? He gave it to me, his one
    gift, but your house
Is a house of thieves. One boy was honest and so you killed him. The boy
    respected his father's possession.
He despised me, he spat me out. Then when I pressed him hard and set fire
    to his body: the heart and soul
I never could reach, they were both stones: he took his hunter's knife in his
    hand, he made the pain
Of the point in his flesh a servant against me. Into his thigh he drove it, he
    laughed and was lame, and triumphed,
And limped into the darkness of death."

                                                      She stood silent, and Cawdor
    remembered his son's lameness
Stumbling under the old man's coffin up the steep hill. He groaned aloud,
    then Fera's face
Gleaming spotted the darkness before his eyes. "I loved him," she said.
    "Love is a trap that takes
The trapper and his game in the same teeth. The first to die has the luck.
    They hang bleeding together.
But you were a mere dupe and a common murderer,
Not love but envy, dupe and fool, what will you do?"
He swayed against the dark hill, "You make the lies,"
He said hoarsely, "must I always believe them?
Time. Time. All my damnation draws
From having done in a haste. What do you want?"
"If I were you
And had your strength I'd kill the woman first,
Then cut out the eyes that couldn't tell my innocent
Boy's head from a calf's to butcher,
And smell my way to the Rock and take the jump."
"I asked you," he said, "because a known devil's
Word is a warning." She came and touched him. "The first's
Easiest," she said, "to kill the woman: the rest
Follows of its own accord." She stroked his face and said
"It is all easy." He took her throat in his hands,
She did not tremble nor flinch; he tightened his fingers

Slowly, as if he were dreaming the thing not doing it,
Then her mouth opened, but the ivory face
Kept its composure still; his fingers closed
A little harder and half checked the hot breath.
Suddenly she clawed at his hands with hers, she cried
"Have pity! I didn't mean it. Oh, Oh, I was lying.
Let me live!" He set her by and ran back to the house,
She heard him sob as he ran.

                              George was alone
In the lamplit room, Cawdor came in and said
"It's nothing," and went up-stairs, his eyes so sunken
That no gleam showed. He shut himself in the room
He used now, where Hood had slept before. George followed
Quietly and saw the crack under the door
Silent of light; he listened and heard no sound.
Then he returned down-stairs. Fera had come in;
She made a smile and passed him and went to her place.

XV

In the morning Cawdor failed to come down; Michal
At length knocked at his door. She listened, trembling,
And got no answer. She opened the door. He stood
Against the window and said "Is it you Michal?
I'm not well. Let me alone." She saw that the bed
Had not been slept in; she could not see his face
Against the shining light but his voice frightened her,
So gentle and forlorn. "Let me bring you some breakfast,
Father?" "No," he said, "no. But there's one thing
You could do for me." "What thing?" "To let me alone.
Nothing else. Nothing else." She saw that his face
Kept turning toward the bed, the eyes and features
Could hardly be seen against the morning light.
She thought he meant to lie down.

                              When Michal had gone
He locked the door, and leaning to the bed whispered:

"She didn't see you. How astonished she'd have been,
She thinks you're hunting in the north." He smiled fondly
And touched the pillow. "You always had fine hair
But now it has grown longer." A sad perplexity
Wrinkled his face; when he drew back his hand
His eyes were again serene. He went to the window
And stood with his back against the light. "From here
I see you the most clearly. Ah no, lie quiet.
You've had a fall," he said shaking, "don't speak.
This puts my eyes in heaven." He stood a long while
And his face darkened. "She keeps begging to die.
Plenty of others want that and make less noise.
It was only a sorrowful joke last night,
I'd not have done it. I made her beg off at least.
But when she squealed I hardly could let go,
My fingers cramped like the arms of breeding toads.
I've lived some months in pain."

                              He listened, and said:
"I know. Thank God. But if you had died, what then?
I had too much foolish pride to throw the game
Because it hurt." He paused and said "I thought
I needed punishment but death's no punishment.
I thought of telling the sheriff": he laughed. "I know him.
And a judge save me? I had to judge myself.
Run to a judge was only running away
From judgment: I thought I'd not do that; shame Michal
And do no good. Running away. I thought the same
Of killing myself. Oh, I've been thinking.
If I'd believed in hellfire I'd have done it
Most nights of the week." He listened, and shook his head.
"No value in needless pain? Oh yet if I lay
As damned with blood as I believed I was
I'd manage somehow. Tit for tat is good sense.
The debt was to myself as well as to you,
And mostly I've paid my debts. Well, I thank God.
This black's turned gray."

Michal had found her brother
Mending iron at the forge, the little shed
Behind the workshop; she'd heard the hammer and found him.
"Have you forgotten your promise?" "Why no," George answered,
"I'll do it for you. I thought you'd change your mind."
She was as pale as if a dear friend's death
Were being sealed in the plot. "Then do it quickly.
I think that father," she said, "is going to be sick.
Our lives perhaps will change, I'll not have time
For trapping squirrels to notch the dreary days
Of the cage with pitiful instants of pleasure." He frowned
And struck the iron, the red darkening, with scales
Of black, and white flecks.

        While George went to the house
For his revolver, Michal climbed up the hill
Weeping; but when he came with death in his hand
She'd not go away, but watched. At the one shot
The great dark bird leaped at the roof of the cage
In silence and struck the wood; it fell, then suddenly
Looked small and soft, muffled in its folded wings.

The nerves of men after they die dream dimly
And dwindle into their peace; they are not very passionate,
And what they had was mostly spent while they lived.
They are sieves for leaking desire; they have many pleasures
And conversations; their dreams too are like that.
The unsocial birds are a greater race;
Cold-eyed, and their blood burns. What leaped up to death,
The extension of one storm-dark wing filling its world,
Was more than the soft garment that fell. Something had flown away. Oh
    cage-hoarded desire,
Like the blade of a breaking wave reaped by the wind, or flame rising from
    fire, or cloud-coiled lightning
Suddenly unfurled in the cave of heaven: I that am stationed, and cold at
    heart, incapable of burning,
My blood like standing sea-water lapped in a stone pool, my desire to the
    rock, how can I speak of you?
Mine will go down to the deep rock.

This rose,
Possessing the air over its emptied prison,
The eager powers at its shoulders waving shadowless
Unwound the ever widened spirals of flight
As a star light, it spins the night-stabbing threads
From its own strength and substance: so the aquiline desire
Burned itself into meteor freedom and spired
Higher still, and saw the mountain-dividing
Canyon of its captivity (that was to Cawdor
Almost his world) like an old crack in a wall,
Violet-shadowed and gold-lighted; the little stain
Spilt on the floor of the crack was the strong forest;
The grain of sand was the Rock. A speck, an atomic
Center of power clouded in its own smoke
Ran and cried in the crack; it was Cawdor; the other
Points of humanity had neither weight nor shining
To prick the eyes of even an eagle's passion.

This burned and soared. The shining ocean below lay on the shore
Like the great shield of the moon come down, rolling bright rim to rim
    with the earth. Against it the multiform
And many-canyoned coast-range hills were gathered into one carven
    mountain, one modulated
Eagle's cry made stone, stopping the strength of the sea. The beaked and
    winged effluence
Felt the air foam under its throat and saw
The mountain sun-cup Tassajara, where fawns
Dance in the steam of the hot fountains at dawn,
Smoothed out, and the high strained ridges beyond Cachagua,
Where the rivers are born and the last condor is dead,
Flatten, and a hundred miles toward morning the Sierras
Dawn with their peaks of snow, and dwindle and smooth down
On the globed earth.

        It saw from the height and desert space of
    unbreathable air
Where meteors make green fire and die, the ocean dropping westward to
    the girdle of the pearls of dawn

And the hinder edge of the night sliding toward Asia; it saw far under
    eastward the April-delighted
Continent; and time relaxing about it now abstracted from being, it saw the
    eagles destroyed,
Mean generations of gulls and crows taking their world: turn for turn in the
    air, as on earth
The white faces drove out the brown. It saw the white decayed and the
    brown from Asia returning;
It saw men learn to outfly the hawk's brood and forget it again; it saw men
    cover the earth and again
Devour each other and hide in caverns, be scarce as wolves. It neither
    wondered nor cared, and it saw
Growth and decay alternate forever and the tides returning.

It saw, according to the sight of its kind, the archetype
Body of life a beaked carnivorous desire
Self-upheld on storm-broad wings: but the eyes
Were spouts of blood; the eyes were gashed out; dark blood
Ran from the ruinous eye-pits to the hook of the beak
And rained on the waste spaces of empty heaven.
Yet the great Life continued; yet the great Life
Was beautiful, and she drank her defeat, and devoured
Her famine for food.

                There the eagle's phantom perceived
Its prison and its wound were not its peculiar wretchedness,
All that lives was maimed and bleeding, caged or in blindness,
Lopped at the ends with death and conception, and shrewd
Cautery of pain on the stumps to stifle the blood, but not
Refrains for all that; life was more than its functions
And accidents, more important than its pains and pleasures,
A torch to burn in with pride, a necessary
Ecstasy in the run of the cold substance,
And scape-goat of the greater world. (But as for me,
I have heard the summer dust crying to be born
As much as ever flesh cried to be quiet.)
Pouring itself on fulfilment the eagle's passion
Left life behind and flew at the sun its father.

The great unreal talons took peace for prey
Exultantly, their death beyond death; stooped upward, and struck
Peace like a white fawn in a dell of fire.

XVI

Cawdor in the room in the house, his eyes fixed
On the empty bed: "Age tells. I've known the time . . .
But now from having fasted a night of sleep
After some bad ones, my eyes have a dazzle in them
So that I sometimes lose your face, then instantly
The trouble returns. I was cut deep:
But never half my deserving." He heard a listener
Lean at the door and the latch move a little;
His face blanked and was still. After long silence
A gentle tapping, and spoken through the shut door:
"I think you are not well: let me in a moment.
Your voice has been going on and on like fever
And now why has it stopped?" Cawdor stood shaking
Like a gray horse tethered short to the fence,
Unable to rear or step back, a serpent rattling
Its passionate sistrum in the lupin by the hooves.
He extended hands toward the bed, his eyes widened
To hold their vision, but as he feared it vanished,
Then he was not able to restrain his hands
From feeling the length of the bed, patting and stroking
Where there was nothing but the smooth coverlet.
He stood and hardened himself, the knocking renewed.
"I have been deceived. It began in the dark,"
He whispered, "and I've dreamed on after dawn.
Men go crazy this way . . . not I. All's black again,
But the dream was sweet. Black, black, black. Ah,"
He said to the door, "keep still!"

                                    The knocking ceased
And steps retreated. Suddenly his black anguish
Compelled him to kneel by the bed. "What shall I do?
Kill that woman? I've promised not to kill

Fly nor stinking beetle. Nor myself: that
Would be a little too easy, I am a murderer
But not a coward yet. Nothing, is hardest to do.
Oh God show me a way. Nothing?" The prayer
And the attitude stiffened his nerves with self-contempt.
He ceased and stood up. "Nor this." Himself was responsible,
Himself must choose, himself must endure. He stood
And looked at the bed, remembering the sweet dream.

More steps came to the door and he drew it open
Before one knocked. Fera said "You are sick,
And I was afraid to come back alone. I brought
Concha Rosas." He looked from one to the other,
"Both my vomits," he said gently. "I'll never
Send you away. This is something." She whispered to him:
"You are in danger. Everyone here . . . knows.
Ask Concha. If you shut yourself up they'll tell; they've been asked;
Only the fear of your face stops them.
Jesus Acanna was asked in Monterey
When he drove in the steers." Cawdor said gently:
"Stay here. I'll keep you with me both days and nights
For a live spark between the eye-lid and the eye.
What ails you to bring good news?" "I knew he was going mad.
Good news? Why, they'll not hang you. I'll be your perfect
Witness to keep you alive. Buried alive
While all the strength you're proud of rots and drops off,
And all the stupid and deceived mind
Tears itself into red strips behind gray
Stones and black iron. Where is it, San Quentin? Oh, kill yourself Cawdor.
You have no better hope." "I am all you say,
Blind, blind, blind dupe," he answered, "but not a coward yet." "My God,
Watch the man cling, Concha. Who'd ever think
That *his* was sweet to live? But it's not love of life,
It's terror of death." He was not listening. He looked
With softened anxious eyes at the bed, his lips
Moved, though he did not speak. She, not in mockery:
"What do you see?" "A face that I know perfectly
Was crushed — what day of the month is it? — three months

And certain days ago, to a red lump
Of sudden destruction: but can you see? — he smiles at me.
I know there is nothing there." Fera laughed, "Concha
Has scuttled away. *I* see his angry eyes
And tumbled light brown hair and bare strong shoulders . . ."
"Yes: his hair." " . . . when I ran in here at dawn,
He lifted himself in the bed like a white sea-lion
Out of the running wave. His breast was bare.
And it was smooth, it was like smooth grooved stone.
You caught me here in the room." Cawdor looked down
And smiled and trembled. "Perhaps if I hadn't come.
Perhaps if I hadn't come." "You were pitiful enough,"
She said, "before. We'd both like to think that.
No, he was straight and true and faithful as light.
Hard as crystal, there was not a spot to hold by.
We two are damned." She watched him shaking
And thought that now he would make some end; but he
Looked downward sideways and said "It has faded now.
You needn't wait, I'll never again do anything
Until I have thought and thought. I'll find a way."
He said in the door, "I thought the woman was with you."
"Concha? She scuttled: I told you." "No, you said nothing."

She followed. When they were on the stair they heard
George's revolver-shot that killed the eagle,
And the quick echo. Cawdor stopped on the stair
And looked at Fera's face. "Why did you turn
So strangely," she said, "what do you see? I fear
You have waited too long already and now your mind
Is helpless among many voices and ghosts.
Kill yourself, Cawdor, and be safe from that,
For soon it will be too late." He said drearily,
"Since you fooled me my ears and eyes have the trick.
But," with a burrowing motion of the head forward,
"I'm not deceived. Not deceived. . . . Who has Hood's rifle?"
"Ah," she answered, "old fox, that hole won't hide you.
He fired because you were coming at him to kill him:
Your guilt's no less." "I lost it," he said, "in the night in the oaks.

I've often looked there, he loved it." They went out-doors
Under the twisted cypress trees and Cawdor said,
"What were you saying? He fired in the air, not at me.
If you were full of eyes you'd find no fault in him."
Fera laughed out, and pointing at the oak on the hill:
"Hurrah, she's done it. That was the shot. Oh, well done Michal.
See if I always fail. The bird shut in a box
Was eating bitter meat for years and now it is blessed. I've been begging her
To make it blessed. Its arm was like mine." "Killed it? I'm sorry," he said,
    "for Michal." Suddenly he ran
To the dim path and climbed. He shouted "George, George"; his heavy
    voice and the echo of his voice battered
Upward between the walls of the canyon.

                              He came to the shelf of earth,
    and hoarse with breathlessness: "More killing?
You dog, have you got Hood's gun?" Michal looked at his face with startled
    wet eyes, George did not speak
But held out the revolver in the flat of his hand. "I forgot that," Cawdor
    said. "Oh Michal, you loved
This brave-eyed thing. You fed it for years." "It was unhappy, father." "By
    God, if you go killing
Unhappiness who'll be left in the houses? Forgive me," he said humbly,
    "I've much to bear." She, trembling:
"Why . . ." she wetted her lips with her tongue . . . "why did you ask about
    Hood's rifle, he wouldn't leave it?"
George, hastily: "His mind's on another matter. You told me to fix the
    branding-iron shafts . . ." Fera had come
Behind Cawdor, and driving her face like an axe between them: "Let him
    confess. He came to confess.
Listen to him for that will deliver his mind, thence he may win
Your eagle's quietness: we used to feel this cage like a black sun shining
    darkness on the canyon.
Now you've put out the sun, you've cured the sky with a gun-shot, nothing
    but a draggled feather-duster
Left in the cage. Let him confess." Cawdor said hoarsely: "I have learned
    that Hood was innocent. This woman

So angered me that I threatened his life in the night. I am dull and easy to
    lie to. Hood went away
Rather than quarrel with the fool his father; he left his rifle under my feet
    by the fire; I lost it;
If I could find it I'd keep it for him." "Ai," Fera cried sharply, "this is no
    good. Wait, that gray face
Will ripen by summer: you can't bear it forever. What did he use, his
    revolver? Even so little
A creature as that is a key to peace." Cawdor said, "Let me see it again."
    George clicked the cylinder
Out of the frame before he handed it to him. Cawdor took and returned it.
    "If I were weak enough
I could find ways, though I am not wise." He saw a knife-edged flake of
    chipped flint or chalcedony
On the earth at his feet; they stood by Fera's father's grave, and the spring
    rains had failed and not grassed it.
Cawdor picked up the Indian-wrought stone. "There were people here
    before us," he said, "and others will come
After our time. These poor flints were their knives, wherever you dig you
    find them, and now I forget
What we came up for. Why do you fix your eyes on me?
For I can neither imagine what I must do
Nor what I should say. You are like shadows." George said "Father:
Send this woman away. This is the bitter fountain, this is your sickness."
    "For the rifle," she answered,
"Acanna has it. Send me away: do: I've a pretty story for strangers, I'll bring
    back eyes
And dig for the old dog's hoard of bones." She said to Cawdor: "Now
    you've grown gentle, you can't eat meat,
But the others know we'd venison Thursday, Jesus Acanna killed it. He says
    that he got his rifle
In Monterey, have you seen the rifle, Michal? You country people have
    quick minds." "Oh, this is nothing,"
Cawdor groaned, "What does Hood want with a gun? He hunts no more.
However . . . do you see the sun?" George took his arm: "Come, let's go
    down." "Now it's due south," he answered,
"And men come home from the starved fields for food.

We'll go and ask him." George made a sign to Michal
So that she stayed behind when the others went down.
And Cawdor, seeing it: "That was well done. I see you now.
A moment ago you were like shadows of moths
When lamplight falls on the earth outside the window.
If I could have caught you I couldn't have held you. Send away sweet Fera?
What should we do without her?" She said: "That flint
Came from an old man's grave you used to despise
For his great weakness; he was the only mind in this ditch;
But now you don't. What's it for, to nick an artery?"
"It is hard," he answered, "and pleasant in the hand.
Last night I threw my knife out of the window
For fear it might use itself of its own accord.
I'd a good dream."

              He saw Acanna among the cypresses
And called him with the old strength of his voice. "I hear that you've got
    Hood's rifle, you found it in the little oaks
Near by the Rock. Oh keep it," he said, "keep it. That's nothing. Kill all
    the deer for Hood has quit hunting,
Buck, fawn and doe. They say they have foot-and-mouth disease
And carry it over the mountain. But if you see a white doe,
That's the worst kind. Cut out her tongue when she drops,
It's poison. . . . You know that I killed him.
You all know it. George knows it. You've been whispering for long,
Watching my face. You've been staunch and not told
For askings: but that was wrong, it makes you accessory.
Now you must ride and tell, don't stay for dinner.
Get meat in the house and eat on the road, for now
I've confessed: if you don't tell you'll be in the same
Sickness with Cawdor. Go. Go." He pushed by him,
And Acanna stood all twisted, as Cawdor's hands
Had left him, unable to move, looking for guidance. At length
George twitched his dead-white face and answered: "Go on.
Do what he says. He has chosen." While they stood, Cawdor
Faced the hill so that his back was toward them and drove
The point of the flint through fold and flesh of each eye
Drawing sidewise on the stroke, so that his sight

Was burst, and blood and water ran down to his feet.
He did not groan, but Fera saw the red stream
Fall by some yellow flowers. She cried "Have you done
Wisely at last? Not with that chip?" He groaned then
But answered nothing. Then George ran to him and saw
The bitter thing he had done, and moved with sudden
Ungovernable pity thrust the revolver
Into his hand. Cawdor said: "What's this? Oh,
This thing. Keep it for cage-birds.
We have other plans. The decent girl my pleasant companion
Has promised to lead me by the hand up to the Rock
And prove our wings." But Fera staggered and said,
Her arms hanging straight down, head drooped, and knees
Bent like weak age: "I am broken. It is finished."
She covered her eyes against him. "My courage is past.
I have always failed." He said, "I'd not have flown down.
I meant to sit up there and think my old thoughts
Until they come to-morrow and take me. It was mere indulgence.
These punishments are a pitiful self-indulgence.
I'd not the strength to do nothing.

                    Be kind to Michal:
But spring's weeping-time. Oh George it was her face
I fell into this darkness to hide myself from.
But when I am taken from the sight of my mountain
It is better to have no eyes. Has Acanna gone?
Your droughty hay-harvest will be a thin sight."
He extended his hands. "Lead me, whoever is here,
Into the house. My head is full of sharp lightnings
And the ground streams and falls under my feet."

HOODED NIGHT

At night, toward dawn, all the lights of the shore have died,
And a wind moves. Moves in the dark
The sleeping power of the ocean, no more beastlike than manlike,
Not to be compared; itself and itself.
Its breath blown shoreward huddles the world with a fog; no stars
Dance in heaven; no ship's light glances.
I see the heavy granite bodies of the rocks of the headland,
That were ancient here before Egypt had pyramids,
Bulk on the gray of the sky, and beyond them the jets of young trees
I planted the year of the Versailles peace.
But here is the final unridiculous peace. Before the first man
Here were the stones, the ocean, the cypresses,
And the pallid region in the stone-rough dome of fog where the moon
Falls on the west. Here is reality.
The other is a spectral episode; after the inquisitive animal's
Amusements are quiet: the dark glory.

EVENING EBB

The ocean has not been so quiet for a long while; five night-herons
Fly shorelong voiceless in the hush of the air
Over the calm of an ebb that almost mirrors their wings.
The sun has gone down, and the water has gone down
From the weed-clad rock, but the distant cloud-wall rises. The ebb whispers.
Great cloud-shadows float in the opal water.
Through rifts in the screen of the world pale gold gleams and the evening
Star suddenly glides like a flying torch.
As if we had not been meant to see her; rehearsing behind
The screen of the world for another audience.

THE BED BY THE WINDOW

I chose the bed down-stairs by the sea-window for a good death-bed
When we built the house; it is ready waiting,
Unused unless by some guest in a twelvemonth, who hardly suspects
Its latter purpose. I often regard it,
With neither dislike nor desire: rather with both, so equalled
That they kill each other and a crystalline interest
Remains alone. We are safe to finish what we have to finish;
And then it will sound rather like music
When the patient daemon behind the screen of sea-rock and sky
Thumps with his staff, and calls thrice: "Come, Jeffers."

WINGED ROCK

The flesh of the house is heavy sea-orphaned stone, the imagination of
    the house
Is in those little clay kits of swallows
Hung in the eaves, bright wings flash and return, the heavy rock walls
    commercing
With harbors of the far hills and the high
Rills of water, the river-meadow and the sea-cloud. You have also, O sleepy
    stones,
The red, the white and the marbled pigeons
To beat the blue air over the pinewood and back again in a moment; and
    the bush-hidden
Killdeer-nest against the west wall-foot,
That is fed from many strange ebbs; besides the woodful of finches, the
    shoring gulls,
The sudden attentive passages of hawks.

NOVEMBER SURF

Some lucky day each November great waves awake and are drawn
Like smoking mountains bright from the west
And come and cover the cliff with white violent cleanness: then suddenly
The old granite forgets half a year's filth:
The orange-peel, egg-shells, papers, pieces of clothing, the clots
Of dung in corners of the rock, and used
Sheaths that make light love safe in the evenings: all the droppings of the
    summer
Idlers washed off in a winter ecstasy:
I think this cumbered continent envies its cliff then.... But all seasons
The earth, in her childlike prophetic sleep,
Keeps dreaming of the bath of a storm that prepares up the long coast
Of the future to scour more than her sea-lines:
The cities gone down, the people fewer and the hawks more numerous,
The rivers mouth to source pure; when the two-footed
Mammal, being someways one of the nobler animals, regains
The dignity of room, the value of rareness.

FIRE ON THE HILLS

The deer were bounding like blown leaves
Under the smoke in front of the roaring wave of the brushfire;
I thought of the smaller lives that were caught.
Beauty is not always lovely; the fire was beautiful, the terror
Of the deer was beautiful; and when I returned
Down the black slopes after the fire had gone by, an eagle
Was perched on the jag of a burnt pine,
Insolent and gorged, cloaked in the folded storms of his shoulders.
He had come from far off for the good hunting
With fire for his beater to drive the game; the sky was merciless
Blue, and the hills merciless black,
The sombre-feathered great bird sleepily merciless between them.
I thought, painfully, but the whole mind,
The destruction that brings an eagle from heaven is better than mercy.

STILL THE MIND SMILES

Still the mind smiles at its own rebellions,
Knowing all the while that civilization and the other evils
That make humanity ridiculous, remain
Beautiful in the whole fabric, excesses that balance each other
Like the paired wings of a flying bird.
Misery and riches, civilization and squalid savagery,
Mass war and the odor of unmanly peace:
Tragic flourishes above and below the normal of life.
In order to value this fretful time
It is necessary to remember our norm, the unaltered passions,
The same-colored wings of imagination,
That the crowd clips, in lonely places new-grown; the unchanged
Lives of herdsmen and mountain farms,
Where men are few, and few tools, a few weapons, and their dawns are
    beautiful.
From here for normal one sees both ways,
And listens to the splendor of God, the exact poet, the sonorous
Antistrophe of desolation to the strophe multitude.

RETURN

A little too abstract, a little too wise,
It is time for us to kiss the earth again,
It is time to let the leaves rain from the skies,
Let the rich life run to the roots again.
I will go down to the lovely Sur Rivers
And dip my arms in them up to the shoulders.
I will find my accounting where the alder leaf quivers
In the ocean wind over the river boulders.
I will touch things and things and no more thoughts,
That breed like mouthless May-flies darkening the sky,
The insect clouds that blind our passionate hawks
So that they cannot strike, hardly can fly.
Things are the hawk's food and noble is the mountain, Oh noble
Pico Blanco, steep sea-wave of marble.

LOVE THE WILD SWAN

"I hate my verses, every line, every word.
Oh pale and brittle pencils ever to try
One grass-blade's curve, or the throat of one bird
That clings to twig, ruffled against white sky.
Oh cracked and twilight mirrors ever to catch
One color, one glinting flash, of the splendor of things.
Unlucky hunter, Oh bullets of wax,
The lion beauty, the wild-swan wings, the storm of the wings."
— This wild swan of a world is no hunter's game.
Better bullets than yours would miss the white breast,
Better mirrors than yours would crack in the flame.
Does it matter whether you hate your . . . self? At least
Love your eyes that can see, your mind that can
Hear the music, the thunder of the wings. Love the wild swan.

ROCK AND HAWK

Here is a symbol in which
Many high tragic thoughts
Watch their own eyes.

This gray rock, standing tall
On the headland, where the sea-wind
Lets no tree grow,

Earthquake-proved, and signatured
By ages of storms: on its peak
A falcon has perched.

I think, here is your emblem
To hang in the future sky;
Not the cross, not the hive,

But this; bright power, dark peace;
Fierce consciousness joined with final
Disinterestedness;

Life with calm death; the falcon's
Realist eyes and act
Married to the massive

Mysticism of stone,
Which failure cannot cast down
Nor success make proud.

SHINE, REPUBLIC

The quality of these trees, green height; of the sky, shining; of water,
a clear flow; of the rock, hardness
And reticence: each is noble in its quality. The love of freedom has been
the quality of western man.

There is a stubborn torch that flames from Marathon to Concord, its
dangerous beauty binding three ages
Into one time; the waves of barbarism and civilization have eclipsed but
have never quenched it.

For the Greeks the love of beauty, for Rome of ruling; for the present age
the passionate love of discovery;
But in one noble passion we are one; and Washington, Luther, Tacitus,
Eschylus, one kind of man.

And you, America, that passion made you. You were not born to prosperity,
you were born to love freedom.
You did not say "en masse," you said "independence." But we cannot have
all the luxuries and freedom also.

Freedom is poor and laborious; that torch is not safe but hungry, and often
requires blood for its fuel.
You will tame it against it burn too clearly, you will hood it like a kept
hawk, you will perch it on the wrist of Caesar.

But keep the tradition, conserve the forms, the observances, keep the spot
sore. Be great, carve deep your heel-marks.
The states of the next age will no doubt remember you, and edge their love
of freedom with contempt of luxury.

FLIGHT OF SWANS

One who sees giant Orion, the torches of winter midnight,
Enormously walking above the ocean in the west of heaven;
And watches the track of this age of time at its peak of flight
Waver like a spent rocket, wavering toward new discoveries,
Mortal examinations of darkness, soundings of depth;
And watches the long coast mountain vibrate from bronze to green,
Bronze to green, year after year, and all the streams
Dry and flooded, dry and flooded, in the racing seasons;
And knows that exactly this and not another is the world,
The ideal is phantoms for bait, the spirit is a flicker on a grave; —
May serve, with a certain detachment, the fugitive human race,
Or his own people, or his own household; but hardly himself;
And will not wind himself into hopes nor sicken with despairs.
He has found the peace and adored the God; he handles in autumn
The germs of far-future spring.

                            Sad sons of the stormy fall,
No escape, you have to inflict and endure: surely it is time for you
To learn to touch the diamond within to the diamond outside,
Thinning your humanity a little between the invulnerable diamonds,
Knowing that your angry choices and hopes and terrors are in vain,
But life and death not in vain; and the world is like a flight of swans.

GRAY WEATHER

It is true that, older than man and ages to outlast him, the Pacific surf
Still cheerfully pounds the worn granite drum;
But there's no storm; and the birds are still, no song; no kind of excess;
Nothing that shines, nothing is dark;
There is neither joy nor grief nor a person, the sun's tooth sheathed in cloud,
And life has no more desires than a stone.
The stormy conditions of time and change are all abrogated, the essential
Violences of survival, pleasure,
Love, wrath and pain, and the curious desire of knowing, all perfectly
    suspended.
In the cloudy light, in the timeless quietness,
One explores deeper than the nerves or heart of nature, the womb or soul,
To the bone, the careless white bone, the excellence.

THE PURSE-SEINE

Our sardine fishermen work at night in the dark of the moon; daylight
   or moonlight
They could not tell where to spread the net, unable to see the
   phosphorescence of the shoals of fish.
They work northward from Monterey, coasting Santa Cruz; off New Year's
   Point or off Pigeon Point
The look-out man will see some lakes of milk-color light on the sea's
   night-purple; he points, and the helmsman
Turns the dark prow, the motor-boat circles the gleaming shoal and drifts
   out her seine-net. They close the circle
And purse the bottom of the net, then with great labor haul it in.

                                                        I cannot
   tell you
How beautiful the scene is, and a little terrible, then, when the crowded fish
Know they are caught, and wildly beat from one wall to the other of their
   closing destiny the phosphorescent
Water to a pool of flame, each beautiful slender body sheeted with flame,
   like a live rocket
A comet's-tail wake of clear yellow flame; while outside the narrowing
Floats and cordage of the net great sea-lions come up to watch, sighing in
   the dark; the vast walls of night
Stand erect to the stars.

                              Lately I was looking from a night mountain-top
On a wide city, the colored splendor, galaxies of light: how could I help
   but recall the seine-net
Gathering the luminous fish? I cannot tell you how beautiful the city
   appeared, and a little terrible.
I thought, We have geared the machines and locked all together into
   interdependence; we have built the great cities; now
There is no escape. We have gathered vast populations incapable of free
   survival, insulated
From the strong earth, each person in himself helpless, on all dependent.
   The circle is closed, and the net

Is being hauled in. They hardly feel the cords drawing, yet they shine
   already. The inevitable mass-disasters
Will not come in our time nor in our children's, but we and our children
Must watch the net draw narrower, government take all powers, — or
   revolution, and the new government
Take more than all, add to kept bodies kept souls, — or anarchy, the
   mass-disasters.

               These things are Progress;
Do you marvel our verse is troubled or frowning, while it keeps its reason?
   Or it lets go, lets the mood flow
In the manner of the recent young men into mere hysteria, splintered
   gleams, crackled laughter. But they are quite wrong.
There is no reason for amazement: surely one always knew that cultures
   decay, and life's end is death.

THE WIND-STRUCK MUSIC

Ed Stiles and old Tom Birnam went up to their cattle on the bare hills
Above Mal Paso; they'd ridden under the stars' white death, when they
  reached the ridge the huge tiger-lily
Of a certain cloud-lapped astonishing autumn sunrise opened all its petals.
  Ed Stiles pulled in his horse,
That flashy palamino he rode — cream-color, heavy white mane, white tail,
  his pride — and said
"Look, Tom. My God. Ain't that a beautiful sunrise?" Birnam drew down
  his mouth, set the hard old chin,
And whined: "Now, Ed: listen here: I haven't an ounce of poetry in all my
  body. It's cows we're after."
Ed laughed and followed; they began to sort the heifers out of the herd.
  One red little deer-legged creature
Rolled her wild eyes and ran away down the hill, the old man hard after her.
  She ran through a deep-cut gully,
And Birnam's piebald would have made a clean jump but the clay lip
Crumbled under his take-off, he slipped and
Spilled in the pit, flailed with four hooves and came out scrambling. Stiles
  saw them vanish,
Then the pawing horse and the flapping stirrups. He rode and looked down
  and saw the old man in the gully-bottom
Flat on his back, most grimly gazing up at the sky. He saw the earth banks,
  the sparse white grass,
The strong dark sea a thousand feet down below, red with reflections of
  clouds. He said "My God
Tom are you hurt?" Who answered slowly, "No, Ed.
I'm only lying here thinking o' my four sons" — biting the words
Carefully between his lips — "big handsome men, at present lolling in bed
  in their ... silk ... pyjamas ...
And why the devil I keep on working?" He stood up slowly and wiped the
  dirt from his cheek, groaned, spat,
And climbed up the clay bank. Stiles laughed: "Tom, I can't tell you: I guess
  you like to. By God I guess
You like the sunrises." The old man growled in his throat and said
"Catch me my horse."

This old man died last winter, having lived
eighty-one years under open sky,
Concerned with cattle, horses and hunting, no thought nor emotion that all
his ancestors since the ice-age
Could not have comprehended. I call that a good life; narrow, but vastly
better than most
Men's lives, and beyond comparison more beautiful; the wind-struck music
man's bones were moulded to be the harp for.

NOVA

That Nova was a moderate star like our good sun; it stored no doubt a little more than it spent
Of heat and energy until the increasing tension came to the trigger-point
Of a new chemistry; then what was already flaming found a new manner of flaming ten-thousandfold
More brightly for a brief time; what was a pin-point fleck on a sensitive plate at the great telescope's
Eye-piece now shouts down the steep night to the naked eye, a nine-day super-star.

It is likely our moderate
Father the sun will sometime put off his nature for a similar glory. The earth would share it; these tall
Green trees would become a moment's torches and vanish, the oceans would explode into invisible steam,
The ships and the great whales fall through them like flaming meteors into the emptied abysm, the six-mile
Hollows of the Pacific sea-bed might smoke for a moment. Then the earth would be like the pale proud moon,
Nothing but vitrified sand and rock would be left on earth. This is a probable death-passion
For the sun's planets; we have no knowledge to assure us it may not happen at any moment of time.

Meanwhile the sun shines wisely and warm, trees flutter green in the wind, girls take their clothes off
To bathe in the cold ocean or to hunt love; they stand laughing in the white foam, they have beautiful
Shoulders and thighs, they are beautiful animals, all life is beautiful. We cannot be sure of life for one moment;
We can, by force and self-discipline, by many refusals and a few assertions, in the teeth of fortune assure ourselves
Freedom and integrity in life or integrity in death. And we know that the enormous invulnerable beauty of things
Is the face of God, to live gladly in its presence, and die without grief or fear knowing it survives us.

THE BEAKS OF EAGLES

An eagle's nest on the head of an old redwood on one of the
    precipice-footed ridges
Above Ventana Creek, that jagged country which nothing but a falling
    meteor will ever plow; no horseman
Will ever ride there, no hunter cross this ridge but the winged ones, no one
    will steal the eggs from this fortress.
The she-eagle is old, her mate was shot long ago, she is now mated with a
    son of hers.
When lightning blasted her nest she built it again on the same tree, in the
    splinters of the thunder-bolt.
The she-eagle is older than I; she was here when the fires of 'eighty-five
    raged on these ridges,
She was lately fledged and dared not hunt ahead of them but ate scorched
    meat. The world has changed in her time;
Humanity has multiplied, but not here; men's hopes and thoughts and
    customs have changed, their powers are enlarged,
Their powers and their follies have become fantastic,
The unstable animal never has been changed so rapidly. The motor and the
    plane and the great war have gone over him,
And Lenin has lived and Jehovah died: while the mother-eagle
Hunts her same hills, crying the same beautiful and lonely cry and is never
    tired; dreams the same dreams,
And hears at night the rock-slides rattle and thunder in the throats of these
    living mountains.

                It is good for man
To try all changes, progress and corruption, powers, peace and anguish, not
    to go down the dinosaur's way
Until all his capacities have been explored: and it is good for him
To know that his needs and nature are no more changed in fact in ten
    thousand years than the beaks of eagles.

OH LOVELY ROCK

We stayed the night in the pathless gorge of Ventana Creek, up the east
    fork.
The rock walls and the mountain ridges hung forest on forest above our
    heads, maple and redwood,
Laurel, oak, madrone, up to the high and slender Santa Lucian firs that
    stare up the cataracts
Of slide-rock to the star-color precipices.

                                    We lay on gravel and kept a
    little camp-fire for warmth.
Past midnight only two or three coals glowed red in the cooling darkness;
    I laid a clutch of dead bay-leaves
On the ember ends and felted dry sticks across them and lay down again.
    The revived flame
Lighted my sleeping son's face and his companion's, and the vertical face of
    the great gorge-wall
Across the stream. Light leaves overhead danced in the fire's breath,
    tree-trunks were seen: it was the rock wall
That fascinated my eyes and mind. Nothing strange: light-gray diorite with
    two or three slanting seams in it,
Smooth-polished by the endless attrition of slides and floods; no fern nor
    lichen, pure naked rock . . . as if I were
Seeing rock for the first time. As if I were seeing through the flame-lit
    surface into the real and bodily
And living rock. Nothing strange . . . I cannot
Tell you how strange: the silent passion, the deep nobility and childlike
    loveliness: this fate going on
Outside our fates. It is here in the mountain like a grave smiling child.
    I shall die, and my boys
Will live and die, our world will go on through its rapid agonies of change
    and discovery; this age will die
And wolves have howled in the snow around a new Bethlehem: this rock
    will be here, grave, earnest, not passive: the energies
That are its atoms will still be bearing the whole mountain above: and I
    many packed centuries ago
Felt its intense reality with love and wonder, this lonely rock.

NIGHT WITHOUT SLEEP

The world's as the world is; the nations rearm and prepare to change; the
   age of tyrants returns;
The greatest civilization that has ever existed builds itself higher towers on
   breaking foundations.
Recurrent episodes; they were determined when the ape's children first ran
   in packs, chipped flint to an edge.

I lie and hear dark rain beat the roof, and the blind wind.

                                                  In the morning
          perhaps I shall find strength again
To value the immense beauty of this time of the world, the flowers of decay
   their pitiful loveliness, the fever-dream
Tapestries that back the drama and are called the future. This ebb of vitality
   feels the ignoble and cruel
Incidents, not the vast abstract order.

                              I lie and hear dark rain beat the
          roof, and the night-blind wind.

In the Ventana country darkness and rain and the roar of waters fill the
   deep mountain-throats.
The creekside shelf of sand where we lay last August under a slip of stars
And firelight played on the leaning gorge-walls, is drowned and lost. The
   deer of the country huddle on a ridge
In a close herd under madrone-trees; they tremble when a rock-slide goes
   down, they open great darkness-
Drinking eyes and press closer.

                         Cataracts of rock
Rain down the mountain from cliff to cliff and torment the stream-bed.
   The stream deals with them. The laurels are wounded,
Redwoods go down with their earth and lie thwart the gorge. I hear the
   torrent boulders battering each other,
I feel the flesh of the mountain move on its bones in the wet darkness.

                                                            Is this
    more beautiful
Than man's disasters? These wounds will heal in their time; so will
    humanity's. This is more beautiful . . . at night . . .

THE BLOODY SIRE

It is not bad. Let them play.
Let the guns bark and the bombing-plane
Speak his prodigious blasphemies.
It is not bad, it is high time,
Stark violence is still the sire of all the world's values.

What but the wolf's tooth whittled so fine
The fleet limbs of the antelope?
What but fear winged the birds, and hunger
Jewelled with such eyes the great goshawk's head?
Violence has been the sire of all the world's values.

Who would remember Helen's face
Lacking the terrible halo of spears?
Who formed Christ but Herod and Caesar,
The cruel and bloody victories of Caesar?
Violence, the bloody sire of all the world's values.

Never weep, let them play,
Old violence is not too old to beget new values.

FOR UNA

I

I built her a tower when I was young—
Sometime she will die—
I built it with my hands, I hung
Stones in the sky.

Old but still strong I climb the stone—
Sometime she will die—
Climb the steep rough steps alone,
And weep in the sky.

Never weep, never weep.

II

Never be astonished, dear.
Expect change,
Nothing is strange.

We have seen the human race
Capture all its dreams,
All except peace.

We have watched mankind like Christ
Toil up and up,
To be hanged at the top.

No longer envying the birds,
That ancient prayer for
Wings granted: therefore

The heavy sky over London
Stallion-hoofed
Falls on the roofs.

These are the falling years,
They will go deep,
Never weep, never weep.

With clear eyes explore the pit.
Watch the great fall
With religious awe.

III

It is not Europe alone that is falling
Into blood and fire.
Decline and fall have been dancing in all men's souls
For a long while.

Sometime at the last gasp comes peace
To every soul.
Never to mine until I find out and speak
The things that I know.

IV

To-morrow I will take up that heavy poem again
About Ferguson, deceived and jealous man
Who bawled for the truth, the truth, and failed to endure
Its first least gleam. That poem bores me, and I hope will bore
Any sweet soul that reads it, being some ways
My very self but mostly my antipodes;
But having waved the heavy artillery to fire
I must hammer on to an end.

                         To-night, dear,
Let's forget all that, that and the war,
And enisle ourselves a little beyond time,
You with this Irish whiskey, I with red wine
While the stars go over the sleepless ocean,
And sometime after midnight I'll pluck you a wreath
Of chosen ones; we'll talk about love and death,

Rock-solid themes, old and deep as the sea,
Admit nothing more timely, nothing less real
While the stars go over the timeless ocean,
And when they vanish we'll have spent the night well.

CASSANDRA

The mad girl with the staring eyes and long white fingers
Hooked in the stones of the wall,
The storm-wrack hair and the screeching mouth: does it matter, Cassandra,
Whether the people believe
Your bitter fountain? Truly men hate the truth; they'd liefer
Meet a tiger on the road.
Therefore the poets honey their truth with lying; but religion-
Venders and political men
Pour from the barrel, new lies on the old, and are praised for kindly
Wisdom. Poor bitch, be wise.
No: you'll still mumble in a corner a crust of truth, to men
And gods disgusting. — You and I, Cassandra.

THE EYE

The Atlantic is a stormy moat; and the Mediterranean,
The blue pool in the old garden,
More than five thousand years has drunk sacrifice
Of ships and blood, and shines in the sun; but here the Pacific: —
Our ships, planes, wars are perfectly irrelevant.
Neither our present blood-feud with the brave dwarfs
Nor any future world-quarrel of westering
And eastering man, the bloody migrations, greed of power, clash of faiths —
Is a speck of dust on the great scale-pan.
Here from this mountain shore, headland beyond stormy headland
    plunging like dolphins through the blue sea-smoke
Into pale sea, — look west at the hill of water: it is half the planet: this dome,
    this half-globe, this bulging
Eyeball of water, arched over to Asia,
Australia and white Antarctica: those are the eyelids that never close; this is
    the staring unsleeping
Eye of the earth; and what it watches is not our wars.

THE BLOOD-GUILT

So long having foreseen these convulsions, forecast the hemorrhagic
Fevers of civilization past prime striving to die, and having through verse,
    image and fable
For more than twenty years tried to condition the mind to this bloody
    climate:—do you like it,
Justified prophet?

        I would rather have died twenty years ago.

               "Sad sons of the
stormy fall,"
You said, "no escape; you have to inflict and endure . . . and the world is like
    a flight of swans."

        I said, "No escape."

           You knew also that your own
country, though ocean-guarded, nothing to gain, by its destined fools
Would be lugged in.

        I said, "No escape."

           If you had not been beaten
beforehand, hopelessly fatalist,
You might have spoken louder and perhaps been heard, and prevented
    something.

      I? Have you never heard
That who'd lead must not see?

         You saw it, you despaired of preventing it, you
share the blood-guilt.

      Yes.

ORIGINAL SIN

The man-brained and man-handed ground-ape, physically
The most repulsive of all hot-blooded animals
Up to that time of the world: they had dug a pitfall
And caught a mammoth, but how could their sticks and stones
Reach the life in that hide? They danced around the pit, shrieking
With ape excitement, flinging sharp flints in vain, and the stench of their
    bodies
Stained the white air of dawn; but presently one of them
Remembered the yellow dancer, wood-eating fire
That guards the cave-mouth: he ran and fetched him, and others
Gathered sticks at the wood's edge; they made a blaze
And pushed it into the pit, and they fed it high, around the mired sides
Of their huge prey. They watched the long hairy trunk
Waver over the stifle trumpeting pain,
And they were happy.

                    Meanwhile the intense color and nobility of
        sunrise,
Rose and gold and amber, flowed up the sky. Wet rocks were shining,
    a little wind
Stirred the leaves of the forest and the marsh flag-flowers; the soft valley
    between the low hills
Became as beautiful as the sky; while in its midst, hour after hour,
    the happy hunters
Roasted their living meat slowly to death.

                        These are the people.
This is the human dawn. As for me, I would rather
Be a worm in a wild apple than a son of man.
But we are what we are, and we might remember
Not to hate any person, for all are vicious;
And not be astonished at any evil, all are deserved;
And not fear death; it is the only way to be cleansed.

TRAGEDY HAS OBLIGATIONS

If you had thrown a little more boldly in the flood of fortune
You'd have had England; or in the slackening
Less boldly, you'd not have sunk your right hand in Russia: these
Are the two ghosts; they stand by the bed
And make a man tear his flesh. The rest is fatal; each day
A new disaster, and at last Vae Victis.
It means Weh den Gesiegten. This is the essence of tragedy,
To have meant well and made woe, and watch Fate
All stone, approach.

                      But tragedy has obligations. A choice
Comes to each man when his days darken:
To be tragic or to be pitiful. You must do nothing pitiful.
Suicide, which no doubt you contemplate,
Is not enough; suicide is for bankrupt shopkeepers.
You should be Samson, blind Samson, crushing
All his foes, that's Europe, America, half Asia, in his fall.
But you are not able; and the tale is Hebrew.

I have seen a wing-broken hawk, standing in her own dirt,
Helpless: a caged captive, with cold
Indomitable eyes and disdain meet death. There was nothing pitiful,
No degradation, but eternal defiance.
Or a sheepfold harrier, a grim, gray wolf, hunted all day,
Wounded, struck down at the turn of twilight,
How grandly he dies. The pack whines in a ring and not closes,
The head lifts, the great fangs grin, the hunters
Admire their victim. That is how you should end — for they prophesied
You would die like a dog — like a wolf, war-loser.

                         (JUNE '43.)

RHYTHM AND RHYME

The tide-flow of passionate speech, breath, blood-pulse, the sea's waves
     and time's return,
They make the metre; but rhyme seems a child's game.
Let the low-Latin languages, the lines lacking strong accents, lean on it;
Our north-sea English needs no such ornament.
Born free, and searaid-fed from far shores, why should it taggle its head
With tinkling sheep-bells, like Rome's slaves' daughters?

ANIMALS

At dawn a knot of sea-lions lies off the shore
In the slow swell between the rock and the cliff,
Sharp flippers lifted, or great-eyed heads, as they roll in the sea,
Bigger than draft-horses, and barking like dogs
Their all-night song. It makes me wonder a little
That life near kin to human, intelligent, hot-blooded, idle and singing, can
     float at ease
In the ice-cold midwinter water. Then, yellow dawn
Colors the south, I think about the rapid and furious lives in the sun:
They have little to do with ours; they have nothing to do with oxygen and
     salted water; they would look monstrous
If we could see them: the beautiful passionate bodies of living flame, batlike
     flapping and screaming,
Tortured with burning lust and acute awareness, that ride the storm-tides
Of the great fire-globe. They are animals, as we are. There are many other
     chemistries of animal life
Besides the slow oxidation of carbohydrates and amino-acids.

THE BEAUTY OF THINGS

To feel and speak the astonishing beauty of things — earth, stone and water,
Beast, man and woman, sun, moon and stars —
The blood-shot beauty of human nature, its thoughts, frenzies and
　　passions,
And unhuman nature its towering reality —
For man's half dream; man, you might say, is nature dreaming, but rock
And water and sky are constant — to feel
Greatly, and understand greatly, and express greatly, the natural
Beauty, is the sole business of poetry.
The rest's diversion: those holy or noble sentiments, the intricate ideas,
The love, lust, longing: reasons, but not the reason.

CARMEL POINT

The extraordinary patience of things!
This beautiful place defaced with a crop of suburban houses —
How beautiful when we first beheld it,
Unbroken field of poppy and lupin walled with clean cliffs;
No intrusion but two or three horses pasturing,
Or a few milch cows rubbing their flanks on the outcrop rock-heads —
Now the spoiler has come: does it care?
Not faintly. It has all time. It knows the people are a tide
That swells and in time will ebb, and all
Their works dissolve. Meanwhile the image of the pristine beauty
Lives in the very grain of the granite,
Safe as the endless ocean that climbs our cliff. — As for us:
We must uncenter our minds from ourselves;
We must unhumanize our views a little, and become confident
As the rock and ocean that we were made from.

DE RERUM VIRTUTE

I

Here is the skull of a man: a man's thoughts and emotions
Have moved under the thin bone vault like clouds
Under the blue one: love and desire and pain,
Thunderclouds of wrath and white gales of fear
Have hung inside here: and sometimes the curious desire of knowing
Values and purpose and the causes of things
Has coasted like a little observer air-plane over the images
That filled this mind: it never discovered much,
And now all's empty, a bone bubble, a blown-out eggshell.

II

That's what it's like: for the egg too has a mind,
Doing what our able chemists will never do,
Building the body of a hatchling, choosing among the proteins:
These for the young wing-muscles, these for the great
Crystalline eyes, these for the flighty nerves and brain:
Choosing and forming: a limited but superhuman intelligence,
Prophetic of the future and aware of the past:
The hawk's egg will make a hawk, and the serpent's
A gliding serpent: but each with a little difference
From its ancestors — and slowly, if it works, the race
Forms a new race: that also is a part of the plan
Within the egg. I believe the first living cell
Had echoes of the future in it, and felt
Direction and the great animals, the deep green forest
And whale's-track sea; I believe this globed earth
Not all by chance and fortune brings forth her broods,
But feels and chooses. And the Galaxy, the firewheel
On which we are pinned, the whirlwind of stars in which our sun is one
    dust-grain, one electron, this giant atom of the universe
Is not blind force, but fulfils its life and intends its courses. "All things are
    full of God.
Winter and summer, day and night, war and peace are God."

III

Thus the thing stands; the labor and the games go on —
What for? What for? — Am I a God that I should know?
Men live in peace and happiness; men live in horror
And die howling. Do you think the blithe sun
Is ignorant that black waste and beggarly blindness trail him like hounds,
And will have him at last? He will be strangled
Among his dead satellites, remembering magnificence.

IV

I stand on the cliff at Sovranes creek-mouth.
Westward beyond the raging water and the bent shoulder of the world
The bitter futile war in Korea proceeds, like an idiot
Prophesying. It is too hot in mind
For anyone, except God perhaps, to see beauty in it. Indeed it is hard to see
    beauty
In any of the acts of man: but that means the acts of a sick microbe
On a satellite of a dust-grain twirled in a whirlwind
In the world of stars. . . .
Something perhaps may come of him; in any event
He can't last long. — Well: I am short of patience
Since my wife died . . . and this era of spite and hate-filled half-worlds
Gets to the bone. I believe that man too is beautiful,
But it is hard to see, and wrapped up in falsehoods. Michael Angelo and
    the Greek sculptors —
How they flattered the race! Homer and Shakespeare —
How they flattered the race!

V

One light is left us: the beauty of things, not men;
The immense beauty of the world, not the human world.
Look — and without imagination, desire nor dream — directly
At the mountains and sea. Are they not beautiful?
These plunging promontories and flame-shaped peaks
Stopping the sombre stupendous glory, the storm-fed ocean? Look at the
    Lobos Rocks off the shore,

With foam flying at their flanks, and the long sea-lions
Couching on them. Look at the gulls on the cliff-wind,
And the soaring hawk under the cloud-stream—
But in the sage-brush desert, all one sun-stricken
Color of dust, or in the reeking tropical rain-forest,
Or in the intolerant north and high thrones of ice—is the earth not
    beautiful?
Nor the great skies over the earth?
The beauty of things means virtue and value in them.
It is in the beholder's eye, not the world? Certainly.
It is the human mind's translation of the transhuman
Intrinsic glory. It means that the world is sound,
Whatever the sick microbe does. But he too is part of it.

THE DEER LAY DOWN THEIR BONES

I followed the narrow cliffside trail half way up the mountain
Above the deep river-canyon. There was a little cataract crossed the path,
   flinging itself
Over tree roots and rocks, shaking the jewelled fern-fronds, bright bubbling
   water
Pure from the mountain, but a bad smell came up. Wondering at it I
   clambered down the steep stream
Some forty feet, and found in the midst of bush-oak and laurel,
Hung like a bird's nest on the precipice brink a small hidden clearing,
Grass and a shallow pool. But all about there were bones lying in the grass,
   clean bones and stinking bones,
Antlers and bones: I understood that the place was a refuge for wounded
   deer; there are so many
Hurt ones escape the hunters and limp away to lie hidden; here they have
   water for the awful thirst
And peace to die in; dense green laurel and grim cliff
Make sanctuary, and a sweet wind blows upward from the deep gorge. —
   I wish my bones were with theirs.

But that's a foolish thing to confess, and a little cowardly. We know that life
Is on the whole quite equally good and bad, mostly gray neutral, and can be
   endured
To the dim end, no matter what magic of grass, water and precipice, and
   pain of wounds,
Makes death look dear. We have been given life and have used it — not a
   great gift perhaps — but in honesty
Should use it all. Mine's empty since my love died — Empty? The
   flame-haired grandchild with great blue eyes
That look like hers? — What can I do for the child? I gaze at her and wonder
   what sort of man
In the fall of the world . . . I am growing old, that is the trouble. My
   children and little grandchildren
Will find their way, and why should I wait ten years yet, having lived
   sixty-seven, ten years more or less,
Before I crawl out on a ledge of rock and die snapping, like a wolf

Who has lost his mate? — I am bound by my own thirty-year-old decision:
    who drinks the wine
Should take the dregs; even in the bitter lees and sediment
New discovery may lie. The deer in that beautiful place lay down their
    bones: I must wear mine.

THE SHEARS

A great dawn-color rose widening the petals around her gold eye
Peers day and night in the window. She watches us
Lighting lamps, talking, reading, and the children playing, and the dogs by
    the fire,
She watches earnestly, uncomprehending,
As we stare into the world of trees and roses uncomprehending,
There is a great gulf fixed. But even while
I gaze, and the rose at me, my little flower-greedy daughter-in-law
Walks with shears, very blonde and housewifely,
Through the small garden, and suddenly the rose finds herself rootless
    in-doors.
Now she is part of the life she watched.
So we: death comes and plucks us: we become part of the living earth
And wind and water we so loved. We are they.

BIRDS AND FISHES

Every October millions of little fish come along the shore,
Coasting this granite edge of the continent
On their lawful occasions: but what a festival for the sea-fowl.
What a witches' sabbath of wings
Hides the dark water. The heavy pelicans shout "Haw!" like Job's warhorse
And dive from the high air, the cormorants
Slip their long black bodies under the water and hunt like wolves
Through the green half-light. Screaming the gulls watch,
Wild with envy and malice, cursing and snatching. What hysterical greed!
What a filling of pouches! the mob-
Hysteria is nearly human — these decent birds! — as if they were finding
Gold in the street. It is better than gold,
It can be eaten: and which one in all this fury of wildfowl pities the fish?
No one certainly. Justice and mercy
Are human dreams, they do not concern the birds nor the fish nor eternal
    God.
However — look again before you go.
The wings and the wild hungers, the wave-worn skerries, the bright quick
    minnows
Living in terror to die in torment —
Man's fate and theirs — and the island rocks and immense ocean beyond,
    and Lobos
Darkening above the bay: they are beautiful?
That is their quality: not mercy, not mind, not goodness, but the beauty of
    God.

VULTURE

I had walked since dawn and lay down to rest on a bare hillside
Above the ocean. I saw through half-shut eyelids a vulture wheeling high up
    in heaven,
And presently it passed again, but lower and nearer, its orbit narrowing,
    I understood then
That I was under inspection. I lay death-still and heard the flight-feathers
Whistle above me and make their circle and come nearer. I could see the
    naked red head between the great wings
Beak downward staring. I said "My dear bird we are wasting time here.
These old bones will still work; they are not for you." But how beautiful
    he'd looked, gliding down
On those great sails; how beautiful he looked, veering away in the sea-light
    over the precipice. I tell you solemnly
That I was sorry to have disappointed him. To be eaten by that beak and
    become part of him, to share those wings and those eyes —
What a sublime end of one's body, what an enskyment; what a life after
    death.

GRANDDAUGHTER

And here's a portrait of my granddaughter Una
When she was two years old: a remarkable painter,
A perfect likeness; nothing tricky nor modernist,
Nothing of the artist fudging his art into the picture,
But simple and true. She stands in a glade of trees with a still inlet
Of blue ocean behind her. Thus exactly she looked then,
A forgotten flower in her hand, those great blue eyes
Asking and wondering.

                Now she is five years old
And found herself; she does not ask any more but commands,
Sweet and fierce-tempered; that light red hair of hers
Is the fuse for explosions. When she is eighteen
I'll not be here. I hope she will find her natural elements,
Laughter and violence; and in her quiet times
The beauty of things—the beauty of transhuman things,
Without which we are all lost. I hope she will find
Powerful protection and a man like a hawk to cover her.

HAND

Fallen in between the tendons and bones
It looks like a dead hand. Poor hand a little longer
Write, and see what comes forth from a dead hand.

OYSTERS

On the wide Texan and New Mexican ranches
They call them prairie oysters, but here on the Pacific coast-range,
Mountain oysters. The spring round-up was finished,
The calves had been cut and branded and their ears notched,
And staggered with their pain up the mountain. A vast rose and gold sunset,
    very beautiful, made in April,
Moved overhead. The men had gone down to the ranch-house,
But three old men remained by the dying branding-fire
At the corral gate, Lew Clark and Gilchrist
And Onofrio the Indian; they searched the trampled
Earth by the fire, gathering the testicles of gelded bull-calves
Out of the bloody dust; they peeled and toasted them
Over the dying branding-fire and chewed them down,
Grinning at each other, believing that the masculine glands
Would renew youth.

            The unhappy calves bawled in their pain and their
        mothers answered them.
The vast sunset, all colored, all earnest, all golden, withdrew a little higher
    but made a fierce heart
Against the sea-line, spouting a sudden red glare like the eye of God. The
    old men
Chewed at their meat.

            I do not believe the testicles of bull-calves
Will make an old man young again, but if they could —
What fools those old men are. Age brings hard burdens,
But at worst cools hot blood and sets men free
From the sexual compulsions that madden youth.
Why would they dip their aging bodies again
Into that fire? For old men death's the fire.
Let them dream beautiful death, not women's loins.

Prose

LETTER TO SISTER MARY JAMES POWER
[October 1, 1934]

Dear Sister Mary James:
Your letter should have been answered sooner, but there have been so many visitors and other events the past fortnight.

As to my "religious attitudes" — you know it is a sort of tradition in this country not to talk about religion for fear of offending — I am still a little subject to the tradition, and rather dislike stating my "attitudes" except in the course of a poem. However, they are simple. I believe that the universe is one being, all its parts are different expressions of the same energy, and they are all in communication with each other, influencing each other, therefore parts of one organic whole. (This is physics, I believe, as well as religion.) The parts change and pass, or die, people and races and rocks and stars, none of them seems to me important in itself, but only the whole. This whole is in all its parts so beautiful, and is felt by me to be so intensely in earnest, that I am compelled to love it, and to think of it as divine. It seems to me that this whole alone is worthy of the deeper sort of love; and that here is peace, freedom, I might say a kind of salvation, in turning one's affection outward toward this one God, rather than inward on one's self, or on humanity, or on human imagination and abstractions — the world of spirits.

I think that it is our privilege and felicity to love God for his beauty, without claiming or expecting love from him. We are not important to him, but he to us.

I think that one may contribute (ever so slightly) to the beauty of things by making one's own life and environment beautiful, so far as one's power reaches. This includes moral beauty, one of the qualities of humanity, though it seems not to appear elsewhere in the universe. But I would have each person realize that his contribution is not important, its success not really a matter for exultation nor its failure for mourning; the beauty of things is sufficient without him.

(An office of tragic poetry is to show that there is beauty in pain and failure as much as in success and happiness.)

— There is nothing here that has not been more feelingly expressed in my verses; but I thought that a plain question deserved a plain answer. — Of course you are welcome to photostat this at your pleasure.

Sincerely yours,
Robinson Jeffers

INTRODUCTION TO *ROAN STALLION,*
TAMAR AND OTHER POEMS
[1935]

My publisher wrote that if I wanted to revise anything, here was my chance, for new plates would have to be made. I thought in a kind of panic, "Of course I ought to revise, but how terrible!" for it is a pleasure to write, but after a thing has been written I hate to see it again; poems are the sort of children that it is delightful to beget, dreary to educate. Yet it seemed clearly a duty. So I made terms with my conscience and my publisher: "If you'll let me off the revising I'll write an introduction instead; that will only take a few hours, the other would take weeks." This is the introduction, a mere conscience-penny.

It might be entitled "Meditation by a Water-main." We used to walk in the Del Monte Forest in the days when it was uninhabited. Near the place where we climbed a fence to enter the woods there was a deep ravine, bridged by the water-main that ran from the dam up the Carmel Valley to the reservoir lake back of Monterey. A wooden trestle supported the big pipe where it crossed the gorge, and this was our bridge into the farther woods; but we had to scramble carefully, for wild bees hived half way over, in the timbers against the pipe. And it was harder coming back; I had to make two crossings then, one to carry the dog, and one with the firewood that we brought home from the forest.

This was twenty-one years ago, and I am thinking of a bitter meditation that worked in my head one day while I returned from the woods and was making my two crossings by the pipe-line. It had occurred to me that I was already a year older than Keats when he died, and I too had written many verses, but they were all worthless. I had imitated and imitated, and that was all.

I have never been ambitious, but it seemed unpleasant just the same to have accomplished nothing, but exactly nothing, along the only course that permanently interested me. There are times when one forgets for a moment that life's value is life, any further accomplishment is of very little importance comparatively. This was one of those times and I can still taste its special bitterness; I was still quite young at twenty-seven.

When I had set down the dog and went back over our bridge for the bundle of firewood my thoughts began to be more practical, not more pleasant. This originality, without which a writer of verses is only a verse-writer, is there any way to attain it? The more advanced contemporary poets were attaining it by going farther and farther along the way that perhaps Mallarmé's aging dream had shown them, divorcing poetry from reason and ideas, bringing it nearer to music, finally to astonish the world with what would look like pure nonsense and would be pure poetry. No doubt these lucky writers were imitating each other, instead of imitating Shelley and Milton as I had done, . . . but no, not all of them, someone must be setting the pace, going farther than anyone had dared to go before. Ezra Pound perhaps? Whoever it was, was *original*.

Perhaps this was the means to attain originality: to make a guess which way literature is going, and go there first. Read carefully your contemporaries, chart their line of advance, then hurry and do what they are going to do next year. And if they drew their inspiration from France, I could read French as well as any of them.

(This was not all quite seriously thought, partly I was just tormenting myself. But a young man is such a fool in his meditations, at least I was; let me say for shame's sake that I have not considered "trends" since turning thirty, nor been competitive either.)

But now, as I smelled the wild honey midway the trestle and meditated the direction of modern poetry, my discouragement blackened. It seemed to me that Mallarmé and his followers, renouncing intelligibility in order to concentrate the music of poetry, had turned off the road into a narrowing lane. Their successors could only make further renunciations; ideas had gone, now meter had gone, imagery would have to go; then recognizable emotions would have to go; perhaps at last even words might have to go or give up their meaning, nothing be left but musical syllables. Every advance required the elimination of some aspect of reality, and what could it profit me to know the direction of modern poetry if I did not like the direction? It was too much like putting out your eyes to cultivate the sense of hearing, or cutting off the right hand to develop the left. These austerities were not for me; originality by amputation was too painful for me.

But — I thought — everything has been said already; there seems to be only this way to go on. Unless one should do like the Chinese with their heavy past: eliminate one's own words from the poem, use quotations from books as the elder poets used imagery from life and nature, make something new by putting together a mosaic of the old. A more promising kind of amputation; one or two noble things might be done that way, but not more, for the trick would pall on Western ears; and not by me, who never could bear the atmosphere of libraries since I escaped from my studious father's control.

I laid down the bundle of sticks and stood sadly by our bridge-head. The sea-fog was coming up the ravine, fingering through the pines, the air smelled of the sea and pine-resin and yerba buena, my girl and my dog were with me . . . and I was standing there like a poor God-forsaken man-of-letters, making my final decision not to become a "modern." I did not want to become slight and fantastic, abstract and unintelligible.

I was doomed to go on imitating dead men, unless some impossible wind should blow me emotions or ideas, or a point of view, or even mere rhythms, that had not occurred to them. There was nothing to do about it.

We climbed the fence and went home through the evening-lighted trees. I must have been a charming companion that afternoon.

This book began to be written three or four years later. I was past my green-sickness by that time, and did not stop to think whether the verses were original or followed a tendency, or would find a reader. Nor have I ever considered whether they deserved to find one.

from FOREWORD TO *THE SELECTED POETRY OF ROBINSON JEFFERS*
[1938]

A good friend of mine, who is also my publisher, wants me to turn this foreword to some account; he says that a number of people have written pro and con about my verses, and it is high time for the author himself to say something. Very likely. But I do not wish to commend or defend them, though sufficiently attacked; and it seems to me that their meaning is not obscure. Perhaps a few notes about their origins may be of interest, to anyone who is interested in the verses themselves.

Long ago, before anything included here was written, it became evident to me that poetry — if it was to survive at all — must reclaim some of the power and reality that it was so hastily surrendering to prose. The modern French poetry of that time, and the most "modern" of the English poetry, seemed to me thoroughly defeatist, as if poetry were in terror of prose, and desperately trying to save its soul from the victor by giving up its body. It was becoming slight and fantastic, abstract, unreal, eccentric; and was not even saving its soul, for these are generally anti-poetic qualities. It must reclaim substance and sense, and physical and psychological reality. This feeling has been basic in my mind since then. It led me to write narrative poetry, and to draw subjects from contemporary life; to present aspects of life that modern poetry had generally avoided; and to attempt the expression of philosophic and scientific ideas in verse. It was not in my mind to open new fields for poetry, but only to reclaim old freedom.

Still it was obvious that poetry and prose are different things; their provinces overlap, but must not be confused. Prose, of course, is free of all fields; it seemed to me, reading poetry and trying to write it, that poetry is bound to concern itself chiefly with permanent things and the permanent aspects of life. That was perhaps the great distinction between them, as regards subject and material. Prose can discuss matters of the moment; poetry must deal with things that a reader two thousand years away could understand and be moved by. This excludes much of the circumstance of modern life, especially in the cities. Fashions, forms of machinery, the more complex social, financial, political adjustments, and so forth, are all ephemeral, exceptional; they exist but will never exist again. Poetry must concern itself with (relatively) permanent things. These have poetic value; the ephemeral has only news-value.

Another formative principle came to me from a phrase of Nietzsche's: "The poets? The poets lie too much." I was nineteen when the phrase stuck in my mind; a dozen years passed before it worked effectively, and I decided not to tell lies in verse. Not to feign any emotion that I did not feel; not to pretend to believe in optimism or pessimism, or unreversible progress; not to say anything because it was popular, or generally accepted, or fashionable in intellectual circles, unless I myself believed it; and not to believe easily. These negatives limit the field; I am not recommending them but for my own occasions.

Here are the principles that conditioned the verse in this book before it was written; but it would not have been written at all except for certain accidents that changed and directed my life. (Some kind of verse I should have written, of course, but not this kind.) The first of these accidents was my meeting with the woman to whom this book is dedicated, and her influence, constant since that time. My nature is cold and undiscriminating; she excited and focussed it, gave it eyes and nerves and sympathies. She never saw any of my poems until it was finished and typed, yet by her presence and conversation she has co-authored every one of them. Sometimes I think there must be some value in them, if only for that reason. She is more like a woman in a Scotch ballad, passionate, untamed and rather heroic, — or like a falcon — than like any ordinary person.

A second piece of pure accident brought us to the Monterey coast mountains, where for the first time in my life I could see people living — amid magnificent unspoiled scenery — essentially as they did in the Idyls or the Sagas, or in Homer's Ithaca. Here was life purged of its ephemeral accretions. Men were riding after cattle, or plowing the headland, hovered by white sea-gulls, as they have done for thousands of years, and will for thousands of years to come. Here was contemporary life that was also permanent life; and not shut from the modern world but conscious of it and related to it; capable of expressing its spirit, but unencumbered by the mass of poetically irrelevant details and complexities that make a civilization.

By this time I was nearing thirty, and still a whole series of accidents was required to stir my lazy energies to the point of writing verse that seemed to be — whether good or bad — at least my own voice.

POETRY, GONGORISM,
AND A THOUSAND YEARS
[1948]

It used to be argued, and I think it is still accepted by many people, that poetry is a flower of racial childhood, and must wither away as civilization advances. For civilization is based on reason and restraint, poetry on imagination and passion; poetry (they say) is dreams, and civilization the daylight that disperses them. This would be an interesting theory if it were true, but there is no truth in it. The greatest Greek poetry, after Homer, was written at the clear and rational summit of Greek civilization, by the Athenian tragic poets in the fifth century B.C.; and then, as civilization declined, Greek poetry declined. It had its revivals, in Sicily, in Alexandria, and these coincided with revivals of civilization. Latin poetry also, though less typical, because the Romans were not originators but cultivators, has a similar history. It flowered at the peak of Roman civilization, in the late republic and early empire, and declined with it. These are but two examples out of many that could be cited, but they are enough to scuttle the supposed rule. They do not reverse it, for actually there is no rule at all; or at least none is discernible. Poetry is less bound by time and circumstance than any other of the arts; it does not need tangible materials; good poetry comes almost directly from a man's mind and senses and blood-stream, and no one can predict the man. It does not need a school nor an immediate tradition; and it does not need, though Whitman said so, "great audiences too." How much of an audience did Keats have in his lifetime?

The present is a time of high civilization rapidly declining; it is not a propitious period for any of the arts; men's minds are a little discouraged, and are too much occupied with meeting each day's distractions or catastrophe. Yet there is no final reason why great poetry should not be written by someone, even to-day. Whether its greatness would be recognized is another question, for greatness is strange, unexpected, and sometimes repellent; but probably it would, in time. What seems to me certain is that this hypothetical great poet would break sharply away from the directions that are fashionable in contemporary poetic literature. He would understand that Rimbaud was a young man of startling genius but not to be imitated; and that *The Waste Land*, though one of the finest poems of this century and surely the most influential, marks the close of a literary dynasty, not the beginning. He would think of Gerard Hopkins as a talented eccentric, whose verse is so overloaded with self-conscious ornament and improbable emotion that it is hardly readable, except by enthusiasts, and certainly not a model to found one's work on, but a shrill note of warning.

Aside from these instances, and to put the matter more fundamentally, I believe that our man would turn away from the self-conscious and naive learnedness, the undergraduate irony, unnatural metaphors, hiatuses and labored obscurity, that are too prevalent in contemporary verse. His poetry would be natural and direct. He would have something new and important to say, and just for that reason he would wish to say it clearly. He would be seeking to express the spirit of his time (as well as all times), but it is not necessary, because an epoch is confused, that its poet should share its confusions. On the contrary, detachment is necessary to understanding. I do not think that Shakespeare mixed Hamlet or Lear into his life, as Byron did Childe Harold; the greater poet saw his creatures objectively, all the way through, but also all the way around; and thus our supposed poet, being distinctly separate from his time, would be able to see it, and to see around it. And I do not think he would give much attention to its merely superficial aspects, the neon lights and tooth-paste advertising of this urban civilization, and the momentary popular imbecilities; these things change every year and presently change out of recognition, but great poetry is pointed at the future. Its author, whether consciously or not, intends to be understood a thousand years from now; therefore he chooses the more permanent aspects of things, and subjects that will remain valid. And therefore he would distrust the fashionable poetic dialect of his time; but the more so if it is studiously quaint and difficult; for if a poem has to be explained and diagrammed even for contemporary readers, what will the future make of it?

There was a seventeenth century Spanish poet named Góngora, a man of remarkable talent, but he invented a strange poetic idiom, a jargon of dislocated constructions and far-fetched metaphors, self-conscious singularity, studious obscurity. It is now only grotesque, but for its moment it was admired in the best circles, and it stimulated many imitators. Then fashion changed, Gongorism was named, and ridiculed, and its poet is now remembered because his name was given to one of the diseases of literature. Euphuism in England had a similar vogue and a similar catastrophe. It seems to me that the more extreme tendencies of modernist verse — and shall I say also of painting and sculpture? — are diseases of like nature, later forms of Gongorism; doctrinaire corruptions of instinct. It is not generally a failure of execution but a collapse of taste — of critical and creative instinct — that brings an art to eclipse. The error in the artist, which perhaps was only momentary and experimental, is echoed with approval by his admirers and a shoal of imitators, so they mislead each other, and gregariousness and snobbery complete the corruption. ("We understand this art, which the ordinary person can only gape at: we are distinguished people.") So the flock gathers sheep. But poetry has never fallen so deep into this bog as painting and sculpture have, and I believe is now pulling out of it. Poetry must use language, which has a resistant vitality of its own; while sculpture (for instance) may sink to fiddling with bits of wire and tin trinkets.

On the other hand, let it be far from me to propose the average educated man as arbiter of poetry or any other art. He has his own perversions of taste or complete nullity, duller than Gongorism. Usually he does not care for poetry — and no harm in that — but alas that he has a deep uneasy respect for it; — he associates it vaguely with "ideals" and a better world, and may quote Longfellow on solemn occasions. This piety without instinct or judgment is a source of boredom, insincerity and false reputations; it is as bad as the delusions of the little groups; it is worse, because more constant. I write verses myself, but I have no sympathy with the notion that the world owes a duty to poetry, or any other art. Poetry is not a civilizer, rather the reverse, for great poetry appeals to the most primitive instincts. It is not necessarily a moralizer; it does not necessarily improve one's character; it does not even teach good manners. It is a beautiful work of nature, like an eagle or a high sunrise. You owe it no duty. If you like it, listen to it; if not, let it alone.

Lately I had occasion to read more attentively the *Medea* of Euripides, and, considering the reverence that cultivated people feel toward Greek tragedy, I was a little shocked by what I read. Tragedy has been regarded, ever since Aristotle, as a moral agent, a purifier of the mind and emotions. But the story of "Medea" is about a criminal adventurer and his gun-moll; it is no more moral than the story of "Frankie and Johnny"; only more ferocious. And so with the yet higher summits of Greek tragedy, the Agamemnon series and the Oedipus Rex; they all tell primitive horror-stories, and the conventional pious sentiments of the chorus are more than balanced by the bad temper and wickedness, or folly, of the principal characters. What makes them noble is the poetry; the poetry, and the beautiful shapes of the plays, and the extreme violence born of extreme passion. That is to say, three times, the poetry: — the poetry of words, the poetry of structure, and the poetry of action. These are stories of disaster and death, and it is not in order to purge the mind of passions, but because death and disaster are exciting. People love disaster, if it does not touch them too nearly — as we run to see a burning house or a motor-crash — and also it gives occasion for passionate speech; it is a vehicle for the poetry.

To return now to the great poet whom we have imagined arising among us at this time. He would certainly avoid the specialists, the Gongorist groups, and he would hardly expect response from the average, the average educated person: then whom should he speak to? For poetry is not a monologue in a vacuum: it is written in solitude, but it needs to have some sort of audience in mind. Well: there has been a great poet in our time, — must I say comparatively great? — an Irishman named Yeats, and he met this problem, but his luck solved it for him. The first half of his life belonged mostly to the specialists, the Celtic Twilight people, the Decadents, even the Gongorists; he was the best among them but not a great poet, and he resented it. He had will and ambition, while Dowson and the others dropped by the wayside. Yeats went home to Ireland and sought in the theater his liberation from mediocrity; and he might possibly have found it there, if he had been as good a playwright as he was a poet. For the theater — unless it is a very little one — cannot belong wholly to a group; it has to be filled if possible; and it does not inevitably belong to the average. When many people together see and hear the thing — if it is fierce enough, and the actors and author can make it beautiful, — it cuts deep. It cuts through many layers. The average person may even forget his education and delight in it, though it is poetry.

But Yeats found in another way his immortality. He was not a first-rate playwright but he had an insuperable will; and when his Ireland changed, he was ready. Suddenly, in that magic time when a country becomes a nation, it was Ireland's good fortune that there was a great poet in Ireland. Her unique need, and his will, had produced him.

But the great poet whom we have imagined would not expect all that luck. He might not have a fighting will, as Yeats did, to push on with time and abide its turnings; or his time might never come. If he should write a great poetic play he would probably never see it staged; for that is a matter of luck, and against the odds. And it is not likely that his country will ever feel the need of a great national poet, as Ireland did; or as Germany did in her stormy awakening, and produced Goethe. Yet our poet must feel (in his own mind I mean) the stimulation of some worthy audience. He will look, of course, to the future. "What do I care about the present," Charles Lamb exclaimed, "I write for antiquity!" But our man will reverse that. It may seem unlikely that he will have readers a thousand years from now, but it is not impossible, if he is really a great poet; and these are the audience whom he will habitually address. If the present time overhears him, and listens too — all the better. But let him not be distracted by the present; his business is with the future. This is not pleasantry; it is practical advice. For thus his work will be sifted of what is transient and crumbling, the chaff of time and the stuff that requires foot-notes. Permanent things, or things forever renewed, like the grass and human passions, are the material for poetry; and whoever speaks across the gap of a thousand years will understand that he has to speak of permanent things, and rather clearly too, or who would hear him?

"But," a young man cries, "what good will it do me to imagine myself remembered after death? If I am to have fame and an audience I want them now, while I can feel them." — It seems to me that the young man speaks in ignorance. To be peered at and interviewed, to be pursued by autograph hunters and inquiring admirers, would surely be a sad nuisance. And it is destructive too, if you take it seriously; it wastes your energy into self-consciousness; it destroys spontaneity and soils the springs of the mind. Whereas posthumous reputation could do you no harm at all, and is really the only kind worth considering.

TO THE AMERICAN HUMANIST ASSOCIATION
[March 25, 1951]

The word Humanism refers primarily to the Renaissance interest in art and literature rather than in theological doctrine; and personally I am content to leave it there. "Naturalistic Humanism" — in the modern sense — is no doubt a better philosophical attitude than many others; but the emphasis seems wrong; "human naturalism" would seem to me more satisfactory, with but little accent on the "human." Man is a part of nature, but a nearly infinitesimal part; the human race will cease after a while and leave no trace, but the great splendors of nature will go on. Meanwhile most of our time and energy are necessarily spent on human affairs; that can't be prevented, though I think it should be minimized; but for philosophy, which is an endless research of truth, and for contemplation, which can be a sort of worship, I would suggest that the immense beauty of the earth and the outer universe, the divine "nature of things," is a more rewarding object. Certainly it is more ennobling. It is a source of strength; the other of distraction.

A CHRONOLOGY OF JEFFERS'
BOOKS OF POETRY

Flagons and Apples, 1912

Californians, 1916

Tamar & Other Poems, 1924

Roan Stallion, Tamar & Other Poems, 1925

The Women at Point Sur, 1927

Cawdor & Other Poems, 1928

Dear Judas & Other Poems, 1929

Descent to the Dead, 1931

Thurso's Landing & Other Poems, 1932

Give Your Heart to the Hawks & Other Poems, 1933

Solstice & Other Poems, 1935

Such Counsels You Gave to Me & Other Poems, 1937

The Selected Poetry of Robinson Jeffers, 1938

Be Angry at the Sun, 1941

Medea, Freely Adapted from the Medea of Euripides, 1946

The Double Axe & Other Poems, 1948

Hungerfield & Other Poems, 1954

The Beginning and the End & Other Poems, 1963

Robinson Jeffers: Selected Poems, 1965

The Alpine Christ & Other Poems, edited by William Everson, 1974

Brides of the South Wind: Poems 1917–1922, edited by William Everson, 1974

Rock and Hawk: A Selection of Shorter Poems, edited by Robert Hass, 1987

The Collected Poetry of Robinson Jeffers, 5 volumes, edited by Tim Hunt, 1988–2001

The Selected Poetry of Robinson Jeffers, edited by Tim Hunt, 2001

The Wild God of the World: An Anthology of Robinson Jeffers, edited by Albert Gelpi, 2003

INDEX OF TITLES